A RAGE
FOR
CHINA

Published simultaneously in Canada by Holt, Rinehart and Winston of Canada, Limited.

Library of Congress Cataloging in Publication Data
Payne, Pierre Stephen Robert, 1911–
    A rage for China.
    1.   China—Description and travel—1949–
2.   Payne, Pierre Stephen Robert, 1911–   I.   Title.
DS711.P38   915.1'04'50924   77-75931
ISBN: 0-03-022886-7

Designer: Kathy Peck

All photographs are by the author, except for the portraits of Mao Tse-tung and Lu Hsün and the tomb of the emperor Wan Li.

Printed in the United States of America
10 9 8 7 6 5 4 3 2 1

A RAGE FOR CHINA

Robert Payne

HOLT, RINEHART and WINSTON
New York

For PATRICIA

CONTENTS

Contents

Shanghai

Notes from a Diary

Tsinan

Tsingtao

Notes from a Diary

Peking

Notes from a Diary

Epilogue: Japan

Index

Illustrations are on pages 83–90, 187–194, and 239–246.

A RAGE
FOR
CHINA

INTRODUCTION

According to the legend, Alexander the Great did not die in Babylon. Instead, he slipped out of his palace and wandered away across the Asian deserts until he reached China and took service as a simple soldier fighting the barbarians pouring over the frontier. One day he was wounded and carried to a farm house. When he recovered, he dug into his pockets for a coin to reward the kind farmer. He found a small gold coin no larger than a fingernail, which bore his own features, and gave it to the farmer. "Strange," murmured the farmer, "that you should have a coin that so much resembles you." Alexander looked at the coin again. "That," he said, "was the other Alexander," and he went jauntily on his way.

I sometimes thought of this story when I returned to China after an absence of thirty years, seeing a country that had changed almost beyond recognition and myself no longer a young student but an aging professor. In those thirty years China had been shaped anew and bore the indelible stamp of Mao Tse-tung, whose power and influence could be felt in every corner of the land. It was the year when all the great leaders of the Chinese Communist Revolution died one after the other—first Chou En-lai, then Chu Teh, then Mao Tse-tung, whose death was heralded by a great earthquake that killed three-quarters of a million people. A year of calamities and disasters that left the Chinese people numbed and confused, and almost rudderless. A year when the Chinese people were learning the hard way that rulers are mortal and that little or nothing had been done to ensure an orderly succession. I had left China when the civil war was still going on, and I returned to it when it sometimes seemed that a civil war might be beginning. In a single generation the wheel was turning full circle.

There are countries and civilizations that possess a strange legendary quality. Like Proteus, they change their shapes and remain the same. I went to China prepared to see a country "that had changed almost beyond recognition," and saw it, but there was also the other China which had changed so little that one had to look hard to see the changes. Communist China was much closer to the China of the emperors than to the chaotic and inefficient rule of Chiang Kai-shek. It was not only that the Chinese Communists ruled from the Forbidden City in Peking but consciously or unconsciously they adopted many of the authoritarian practices of the emperors and were impelled to follow customs and habits derived from the imperial past. They thought of themselves as men dedicated to the discovery of a new society and the more they spoke of its newness, the more they found themselves repeating ancient history. What was new was sometimes very old indeed, and what they thought was very old and decaying was sometimes very new.

I had met Mao Tse-tung, Chu Teh, and Chou En-lai, and

2

was among the first to say that no power on earth could prevent them from conquering China. They were three superbly gifted men passionately devoted to a cause that went far beyond the classic Marxist interpretation of social revolution. They possessed a human grace and dignity; they were contemptuous of danger, indifferent to comfort, and determined to lead China out of the long darkness of oppression. They knew where they were going and they had an enviable directness of aim. In the battle of wills between the Chinese Communists and the Kuomintang I had no doubt who would be the winner. Once talking with Mao Tse-tung in Yenan in 1946 I asked him what he would do if the Kuomintang tanks entered this small cave-city that was not far from Sian, where the Kuomintang had a large army. He answered: "We will tear them apart with our bare hands." It was this attitude of unconquerable defiance that made it possible to believe the Kuomintang was doomed.

In those days their strength was in having nothing: they had neither armaments nor motorized transport, neither money nor oil nor any of the necessities of modern warfare. They had no stocks of rubber, no iron foundries, no machinery, for all the machines in the territories they captured were taken away by the Russians. They had a small radio station on top of one of the Yenan hills, operated by batteries and when these failed by a foot-treadle that generated a pathetically small supply of electricity. I asked how far the messages would reach. "Perhaps fifty miles, perhaps forty," the head of the radio station replied. "Then how do you communicate with a Communist army two thousand miles away?" I asked. "With patience," he answered. He meant that the messages went slowly from one homemade radio station to another until they stretched across the whole of China. "We have time on our side," he went on. "We are in no hurry, and besides our armies know what to do."

I said that the Chinese Communists had no motorized transport. This is not quite true. In Yenan there were two American jeeps, one of them captured from the Kuomintang, the other bought in Peking and transported on donkey-back across the mountains, after being broken down into its separate pieces. These jeeps were used only on important occasions. One day the extremely generous chief of staff of the Chinese Communist army lent me one of the jeeps and a driver to explore the Yenan Valley. We were returning from the expedition when the jeep went over a small cliff, landing on some black pigs foraging below. We were thrown clear, but the jeep's axle was bent beyond repair. There remained in the capital of Communist China only one jeep.

In retrospect we see now that Yenan formed part of the heroic age of the Chinese Communists. It was the time when they had no weapons except those they wrested from the enemy, and no fear. They were drunk with the righteousness of their cause, and they fed on the legends of the Long March, which was still so close to them that they would speak about it as though it happened yesterday. Very few visitors from abroad came to Yenan, for the simple reason that the Kuomintang government did everything possible to see that the blockade was maintained. While I was there, the only other foreigner was an American-Hawaiian colonel, the sole survivor of YOG, the Yenan Observer Group, consisting of about a dozen Americans sent up to Yenan in 1942 to appraise the military efficiency of the Red Army. Now the Americans had withdrawn, leaving the solitary colonel to report on events in that beautiful valley, where nothing seemed to be happening. Over his cave he raised the American flag every morning and lowered it every evening. Once a week a DC-3 flew from Peking to Yenan with a trickle of supplies that included some medicines and some films but no military equipment. The American colonel was lonely and wished he was with his wife in Honolulu.

In theory Yenan was encircled; so in theory were all the other Communist areas in China. The Chinese Communists claimed that about a quarter of China including nearly all the villages was in their hands. It was a claim that some people who did not know the Chinese villages thought laughable.

The Kuomintang had a healthy fear of the Chinese Communists. They were aware that something very strange was happening in Yenan, something that could scarcely be put into words. It had become a legend, a battle cry, a place of refuge, a generator of power all the more mysterious because no visible power emanated from it. The longer it endured, the more powerful it became. It did not have to do anything; it only had to exist in order to generate more and more power. Students flocked to it from all over China, at the risk of being shot by Kuomintang agents manning the invisible frontier. It had a university, a symphony orchestra, a hospital, a foreign office made of mat-sheds, and a small theater for showing Chinese opera. The university was housed in a series of caves; so was the hospital. There were no streets, for the ancient city was nothing but charred ruins after a succession of Japanese bombing raids. There was only the yellow valley with a small stream flowing through it. In summer you could walk over the stream; in winter it became a raging torrent. High above the valley on one of the hills was a yellow pagoda built in the Sung dynasty. The gods in the pagoda were losing their stuffing and falling to pieces. In the Sung dynasty and long before, Buddhist monks had carved out a cave temple called the Cave of the Ten Thousand Buddhas because so many representations of Buddha were sculptured on the walls. The Chinese Communists used the cave to house a printing press.

In this valley with its sandy floor and loess hills life went on quietly and peacefully. A horse would raise a cloud of dust twenty feet high, a jeep would raise a cloud of dust to a hundred feet before it fell slowly to earth. The sky was a deep blue, the earth yellow, and a red cloth, hung over the mouth of a cave a mile away, would immediately attract attention as though its very existence controverted the laws of nature that said that everything must be yellow, the bright yellow of the tiles on the palaces in Peking. And sometimes other laws of nature were controverted. By natural law the valley was very quiet. Sometimes there came a low humming like a chorus of bees. A bomber or a spotter plane from Sian had been sent up to see whether there was anything to bomb or to photograph, but in fact there was nothing to photograph and nothing to bomb. The spotter plane could not see into the caves or guess the intentions of the Chinese Communist leaders; there were no long columns of tanks and trucks to be photographed. Nor could it observe the one thing that was most important about Yenan: that it was a legend in its own right and a symbol of the massive resistance of the Chinese people to the Kuomintang leadership, and had no real existence outside the human imagination. Yenan was composed of dreams, dust, sand, and shadowy caves. There was nothing the airplanes could do to us, and the Chinese Communists, without airplanes and without anti-aircraft guns, could do nothing to them. Yenan and the airplanes existed independently in different worlds.

For me Yenan was Communist China. Within a few years Yenan became a backwater, for Communist China expanded prodigiously. The men in the caves who looked like weather-beaten peasants and apologized for their cane-bottomed chairs and simple fare took up residence in the Forbidden City in Peking and ruled by decree like the emperors of the past. They had already worked out their program: there would be no landlords, no capitalists, no taxes, no poor and no rich. All this came about much faster than anyone had expected. Out of the Yenan caves the storm arose with extraordinary power and violence, blowing the Kuomintang off the mainland. China was ruled by the survivors of the Long March, stern men with serious purposes, and among those purposes was to root out every trace of the corruption that had sapped the energy of the country for nearly a hundred years. When Mao Tse-tung proclaimed the founding of the People's Republic of China in October 1949, he was proclaiming that for the first time since the Arrow War of 1856 China was master of herself. No longer would she be forced to pay tribute to foreign powers; no foreign concessions with extraterritorial privileges would be permitted to exist on Chinese soil; no gunboats would be permitted to sail up her rivers. A new age of Chinese history was beginning. The dragon which had been so long dormant, suffocating in its own coils, had uncoiled and was wide awake.

One day in Yenan I talked with Mao Tse-tung about the uses and abuses of power. I quoted the old saying of the philosopher Lao Tzu that "government should be as easy as cooking little fishes." He said that was the kind of government he wanted to bring to China. The hand of the government would weigh very lightly on the people. The people would discuss every issue, they would elect their representatives and send them to Peking, many parties would be permitted to exist, there would be no constraints. The entire landlord class would be dissolved, and this would come about quite easily, because the title deeds of their estates would be destroyed and they would no longer have any claim to their property. Capitalists would no longer be permitted to accumulate financial power, but the changeover from capitalism to communism would take place slowly in order not to wreck the economy. He said it would take ten years before the Chinese Communists would possess effective power in China and perhaps it would take longer; and he did not expect to see it happening in his lifetime. He did not want personal power. He wanted the people to have power. "We must trust the people—only the people," he said. All over China there would be meetings and the decisions reached at these meetings would give the government an understanding of what was happening in the people's minds. Government would come up from below. There would be no highhanded orders from above. It would be necessary to work out safeguards in case the government exceeded its authority.

We know that power corrupts and absolute power corrupts absolutely. Lu Hsün, a Chinese writer whom Mao Tse-tung once proclaimed to be "the standard-bearer of our age," once wrote that he had never encountered a government official or a bureaucrat who was not in some way corrupted by power. A man with power, however honest, however humane, is subtly poisoned by it. Once he has it, he seeks to ensure that he continues in full possession of it, even when it is beyond reason. Power is a drug, and every man possessing it is a drug addict. "The strongest poison ever known," wrote William Blake, "is Caesar's laurel crown."

Looking at China from abroad, it seemed to me that the Chinese Communist party had not always avoided the corruptions of power. Inevitably it created an army of bureaucrats; inevitably it became monolithic. The personal power of Mao Tse-tung exceeded the power of the emperors, his directives being regarded as though they were imperial rescripts. No one in history, not even Stalin, had received so much adulation. His portrait hung in every house, in every room. His little red book was in every hand and consulted in every emergency. He was deified in his lifetime. The government of China became the rule of the deified emperor. The people, who remained loyal to him because he was the chief architect of the victory over the Kuomintang, came to possess less and less power, while the faceless bureaucrats of the party ruled in his name. Increasingly, as he grew older, he became remote and withdrawn from the people. For the last twelve years of his life he made no speeches, while his directives often took the form of single sentences uttered in a quavering voice. His wife, Chiang Ching, interpreted these directives in her own manner and to her own advantage. This was not the kind of government he had envisaged during the heroic days in Yenan.

When he died in the early autumn of 1976, he left China in disarray. He left no testament; his appointed successor was little known; the monolithic state, which survived his death, was still in the hands of the bureaucrats he detested so much that he attempted to fight them to a standstill during the Great Proletarian Cultural Revolution. Nevertheless they remained, regarding themselves rightly or wrongly as instruments of his will.

Within a month of his death Chiang Ching was under arrest, and it was widely believed that she had made an unsuccessful bid for supreme power. Drawings and caricatures of her were pasted on a million walls; she was publicly reviled and denounced in the newspapers and at meetings all over China. At the same time her husband,

Mao Tse-tung, was being extolled as the greatest of all Chinese heroes, the wisest of philosophers, and the man whose name would be remembered with gratitude for ten thousand years. Strangely, during this period, there were few Chinese who seemed to realize that something had gone terribly wrong and that the greatest wrong lay in the fact that the people had no voice in their own affairs. "We must trust the people—only the people," Mao Tse-tung had once said. In his last years he had not trusted them; he allowed himself to become a father-image, the supreme arbiter, the deified emperor who demands abject submission to his desires. The wheel turned full circle: the young revolutionary became the old despot.

In the following pages I have described a journey through China during that tragic winter. I have been concerned as much with politics as with the myriad aspects of the journey. Landscapes, ideas, faces, conversations, the shapes of cities, the colors of schools and museums, the carvings in Buddhist temples, the morning mists in Tsingtao and the snow falling on Peking all have their place in the mosaic. I have called this book *A Rage for China* to suggest an overwhelming affection for that beautiful land and also to suggest the dismay of the Chinese people at seeing their country at the mercy of historical forces they could rarely understand.

HONG KONG

The Nine Dragons

I had thought Hong Kong was an imaginary city until I
stayed in the strange ugly building of the Young Men's
Christian Association in Kowloon, facing the waterfront
and the harbor full of ships and the island of Hong Kong
lying only a mile away across the straits, vanishing in the
mist, and looking for all the world as though it was part
of the wreckage of China and was floating away in the
South China Sea. In the YMCA the paint was flaking, the
springs were eating their way through the overstuffed
armchairs, and the fly-spotted oleographs had been handed
down from the Victorian age. The travel agent had promised us that the YMCA would have all the comforts and
conveniences of a modern hotel, but it had nothing of the
kind. We were twenty-four Americans on a friendship
tour of the People's Republic of China, exhausted after a
long journey which had taken us from New York to
Toronto, Vancouver, Anchorage, and Tokyo, and so to
the airfield on Kowloon. No doubt there are simpler ways
of reaching China. And as we stood in the lobby of the

YMCA, surrounded by our mountains of luggage and waiting interminably for the desk clerk to decide what to do with us, we looked like refugees from a storm, with lined faces and crumpled clothes, feeling that we had come to the end of our resources and if we were sensible we would immediately turn around and fly back to New York.

It was one of those hotels where you expect to find seedy Somerset Maugham characters who have abandoned life on the rubber plantations of Malaya for the fleshpots of Hong Kong. The hotel and everyone in it was obviously fictitious; we ourselves were fictitious. Yet no novelist could have invented the hotel and it was beyond imagination that a novelist could have invented the oddly discordant group, apparently chosen by chance, now washed onto the outer shores of China. There were young American Marxists eager to explore the promised land, a number of staid schoolteachers, an ophthalmologist from Texas, a television repairman, a town planner, a retired professor, a biochemist, two doctors, an intelligent representative of International Business Machines, and a few spear carriers for lost causes. There were two blacks and a lady from India who sometimes went off into gales of laughter and could not stop. There was a young editor from the New York weekly magazine *The Guardian* who was described as the group leader and did in fact lead so gently that no one was aware of it. There were those who were passionately convinced of the rightness of the Chinese Communist cause and those who were lukewarm, or came as sightseers, or wanted to get away from home. It was an incongruous and unwieldy group which obstinately refused to be regarded as a group to the surprise later of our Chinese guides who were inclined to think of us as an undisciplined mob. Team spirit was lacking. We were twenty-four vagrants from America with twenty-four sets of opinions.

Our guides thought it incomprehensible that so many opinions could exist.

In Hong Kong we had no guides and wandered where we pleased. We wandered into the Peninsula Hotel, magnificently ornate, all white and gold, the bellboys dressed like admirals, and the forecourt crowded with a dozen chocolate-colored Rolls-Royces ready at any moment to take the hotel guests wherever they desired. By a curious irony the Peninsula Hotel and the YMCA building stood next to one another and seemed to be engaged in a perpetual dialogue. Some of us spent a day in the shops, buying instant clothes (NEW SUITS 24 HOURS), watches, cameras, and we would have bought miniature television sets if we had thought there was one chance in a million of bringing them into China. We explored the honky-tonks of Nathan Road from the outside, noting that topless and bottomless dancing girls were in voluminous supply, and it occurred to us that in all of China there was not one single topless and bottomless dancing girl for sale. We crossed the ferry and examined the myriads of skyscrapers, wondering at the audacity of the architects to charge a fee for designing so many buildings without granting them any character. The Hong Kong and Shanghai Banking Corporation building stands next door to the Bank of China owned by the Chinese Communist government. Both are guarded by lions, but they are lions with a difference. The two lions guarding the Bank of China are carved in white marble; they have mouths like mailboxes and small eyes under backward-sloping foreheads, and their hair is coiled prettily. They look playful and would do no harm to anyone. The two Hong Kong and Shanghai Banking Corporation lions are considerably less playful. They are made of bronze; they are ferocious in the imperial manner with huge glaring eyes and sharp talons; and one is roaring with his mouth wide open and the other has a closed mouth to suggest that the bank will never reveal its customers' secrets. These bronze lions are polished daily until they gleam like silver. They have some claim to be regarded as works of art, while the Chinese lions resemble toys or bookends.

These lions do not tell the true story. The Hong Kong and Shanghai Banking Corporation prints its own bank notes and dominates the economic life of Hong Kong, but its days are numbered. Soon enough the flamboyant entrance will be boarded up and there will be a notice: SUB-BRANCH OF THE BANK OF CHINA. ENTRANCE NEXT DOOR. The Bank of China also prints its own bank notes.

Both banks face Statue Square. I expected to see a statue of Queen Victoria. Instead there is the statue of someone considerably more important to the life of Hong Kong than the queen and empress who once ruled over it. This is Sir Thomas Jackson, who stands in a long bronze frock coat on a high plinth, looking absurdly commonplace, looking in fact like the manager of a small and lowly bank somewhere in the outskirts of London. There was not the least trace of imperial grandeur in his appearance. On the bronze plaque there is written:

In Memory of

Sir THOMAS JACKSON, Bart.
1841–1915

And in grateful remembrance of his
eminent services to
The Hong Kong and Shanghai
Banking Corporation
Whose destiny he guided as chief
manager from 1876 *to* 1902

In front of the statue and all round it there are huge upended and pointed slabs of concrete to prevent anyone from approaching too closely. He is well protected. It would be difficult to throw paint across a fifteen-foot tank trap. I wondered why they did not simply surround the statue with barbed wire.

In the distance lay Kowloon across the blue and silvery straits. Kowloon means "Nine Dragons," and a pleasant story is told about an emperor who came from Peking to visit this forgotten corner of China. He asked the name of the small humpbacked mountains he saw in the distance. "They are the Nine Dragons," his minister said. "But I see only eight mountains," the emperor said. "You, my lord, are the Ninth Dragon," said the courtly minister.

The View from the Peak

Like many people I come to each new city with a feeling of apprehension. For the first day I am lost, like someone who has been spun around twenty times and then ordered to walk along a chalked line. I am drunk with the misery of trying to find my bearings. At the end of the first day I am beginning to recognize the main roads, shops, monuments, museums, post offices. Lines of force, like the patterns made by iron filings when they are magnetized, begin to appear. The processes of adaptation are made easier if the city has a visible center. But Hong Kong has no center and no circumference. There are islands, mountains, Kowloon, the New Territories, Victoria, Aberdeen, Repulse Bay, skyscrapers, sampans and ocean liners, a vast watery jungle. It occurred to me that the best plan was to take the tram to the Peak and look at it from above.

Like a child's toy the small tram lurches and rattles up the side of the mountain on Hong Kong Island at an angle of forty-five degrees, traveling at a speed of about eight miles an hour. You know you are drunk because the skyscrapers at the foot of the island fall away at absurd angles and the fat banana trees are oddly tip-tilted. In theory the tram cannot fall backward because fist-sized cogs fall into place at exactly the right moment, but theory is not very comforting when the tram shakes to a violent halt at one of the four wayside stations and sends you sprawling. You observe that the tram is lightly constructed and would be quickly shattered into matchwood if it fell down the hill. Perhaps, after all, it would be safer to walk, but the mountain is covered with thick scrub and there are no pathways. At the top there is a glass-walled restaurant in the modern style where you can happily drink a glass of whiskey and look out at one of the mysteries of our age. You see the city of Victoria below, where skyscrapers grow like cactuses, and then there is a narrow stretch of sea, and beyond this lies Kowloon, and beyond Kowloon lies the New Territories, and beyond the New Territories lie the rippling blue mountains of China in the misty distance. And then you remind yourself that an exact equivalent to this strange situation could be found if an international port of vast wealth and power, with cheap labor and massive industries, was located on a small island in the Gulf of Finland and if in addition about four hundred square miles of Soviet territory near the island had been leased to its capitalist rulers.

From the Peak many things become clear immediately, and what is most abundantly clear is that Hong Kong, Kowloon, and the New Territories are defenseless simply because they are so very small compared to the enormous bulk of China, which stretches as far as the eye can see. The dragon has only to shake his tail, and all this conglomeration of power and wealth will be swept into the sea. One can imagine a young Chinese soldier coming to Hong Kong in a rowboat flying the red flag with the yellow stars. He is unarmed, he carries no documents, and his cap with the metallic red star is perched jauntily on his head. He smiles as he says: "I have come to accept your surrender." And immediately Hong Kong surrenders and the foreigners pack their bags and go home, as they went home when the Communist troops entered Shanghai.

From the Peak you become aware that Hong Kong is insubstantial, dreamlike. It is an act of the imagination more than a reality. It feeds on the wealth of China, but it also feeds on the human imagination, for it has invented itself. Hong Kong exists by permission of the Chinese, but that permission has never been openly granted and may be rescinded at any time without warning, without official notification. The Chinese benefit substantially by trading with Hong Kong, thus following the capitalist road. The British and the Chinese living in Hong Kong are well aware of the contradictions of the situation, and are not alarmed, for they are both pragmatists and accept the fact that life is full of contradictions. It is even possible that the Chinese Communists will come to realize that there are advantages in combining the *laissez faire* economics of the nineteenth century with the industrial techniques of the twentieth century, thus producing a tolerable society. It is also possible that when the Chinese soldier reports to Peking: "They have all gone. What do we do now?" he will be told: "Tell them to come back again."

Journey into the Interior

When we left Hong Kong for China, we knew we were entering a strange country where nearly all the forms of human civilization as we know them were in abeyance. It was a country of eight hundred million people, and not one of them owned an automobile. There were no landlords, no funeral directors, no lawyers, no priests, no doctors who charged extortionate fees. There was no desperate poverty and no unemployment. The rents were so low that no one had any difficulty paying them, and the shops were full of consumer goods priced so cheaply that everyone could afford them. No pornographic films were shown, there were no prostitutes, and consequently there was no venereal disease. There was no night life, and there were no fashions, for everyone dressed alike. There was no external debt and no inflation, and a visit to a hospital cost only a few cents. Education at all levels was a charge on the government and students paid only nominal fees.

All this was true, but it was not the whole truth. The Chinese Communists have solved many of the most urgent problems confronting the modern state, but there are still many problems left unresolved. They have sometimes solved problems drastically without regard to the consequences, like a surgeon who finds an infected tooth and cuts away the whole jawbone.

They claim they have solved problems that the leaders of the Soviet Union have failed to solve, and they point to Russia as a country that has taken the capitalist road, a statement that sometimes surprises the Russians. In their propaganda the Chinese Communists were inclined to suggest that under the benevolent rule of Chairman Mao Tse-tung they have come closer to an egalitarian paradise than any nation on earth. We wanted to see how many of their claims were true. In the train going to the frontier we had the curious feeling that we were entering an uncharted world. It was the winter of the year that had seen vast upheavals in China; the cauldron was boiling over again; we had come in time to see the emergence of the new dispensation. Or so we told ourselves, gazing at our newly stamped visas, clutching our notebooks, and seeing that our cameras were in order. We were in a mood of high expectancy and prepared for anything—machine guns in the streets or the calm that you see in a Chinese painting.

The pleasantness, the ordinariness of the journey to the frontier, was somewhat disconcerting. Peaceful villages, no armed guards anywhere, lakes and inlets, rice fields and sugarcane. The train chugged along at thirty miles an hour, stopping at every wayside station. Villages we had never heard of with names like Mong Kok, Shatin, Tai Po, Fanling, Sheungshui were strewn across the New Territories. They were all inhabited by Chinese and there was not a single Englishman in sight. In theory and perhaps in practice all these villages were ruled by colonial administrators in Hong Kong, who very carefully avoided using the word *colonial* and had long ago obliterated from their memories the words *Crown Colony*. What was startling was the realization that these Chinese peasants were the subjects of Queen Elizabeth II and if they engaged in litigation they had the right to appeal to her Privy Council. Hopefully the litigation would not continue for many years, since in 1997 the New Territories will revert to China by the terms of a treaty solemnly signed by both powers, and the litigants would have to start all over again.

So here in the New Territories, with the blue mountains of China in the background, the Union Jack fluttering from the flagpoles, and Chinese boys riding on the backs of black buffaloes or herding black pigs or sauntering along the edges of the rice fields, you have the feeling that everything is normal, healthy, and sensible, that nothing will change in the best of all possible worlds, but in fact the entire situation is abnormal and change is inevitable. The New Territories is a kind of no-man's-land. The palms wave, the banana trees rustle their leaves, the ducks waddle in the ponds, blue shadows creep over the landscape, and the earth smiles. Then you remember that this is a tinderbox, where anything can happen. One of the things that could happen is that someone might try to put guns and hand grenades in your luggage in the hope that you will be able to smuggle them safely into Communist China. The China Travel Service is well aware of this possibility and gives you a little leaflet before you leave your Hong Kong hotel.

Attention Please

Due to Hong Kong's peculiar environment and for your safety, kindly examine carefully the contents of your luggage whether there is anything not belonging to you put in by unknown persons without your knowledge, and to have the luggage properly locked before leaving your hotel for the railway station. This applies to any luggage that may be carried by yourself or those which you entrust to our care on the way to Shum Chun.

This leaflet probably needs a commentary. What exactly is meant by "Hong Kong's peculiar environment"? Who are the "unknown persons" who slip things into your luggage? The language is made deliberately obscure. Are they talking about Kuomintang secret agents from Taiwan? The CIA? The Russians? All of these? The leaflet provides the appropriate note of apprehension.

Meanwhile there are the duck farms, the dairy farms, the chicken runs and pigsties all set in a delectable land that might be taken for paradise, so green and peaceful it is. The Chinese wandering in the fields might have stepped out of nineteenth-century prints. Paradise is the gift of a small pink railroad ticket which reads in Chinese and English: *Kowloon to Lo Wu First Class Single Fare*

$3.95, which is not expensive for a two-hour journey. Lo Wu is the last station on the British side of the frontier. Then comes the famous iron bridge over a steep-sided creek filled with wild flowers and shaded by banana trees; you walk over it, and beyond the bridge you enter another town and another planet.

The journey across the bridge is mercifully short, for you have to carry your own luggage. Halfway across the bridge you come upon two large inscriptions, which confront and nicely balance one another: LONG LIVE THE GREAT UNITY OF THE PEOPLE OF THE WORLD and LONG LIVE THE PEOPLE'S REPUBLIC OF CHINA. If you care to ponder these inscriptions in white letters against a blood-red background, you may reflect that the concept of the great unity goes back to the earliest Chinese philosophers and is probably as old as China herself, while the People's Republic of China came into existence only a few years ago. Here, at the very beginning of the journey into China, the very ancient and the very new confront one another. On one side of the bridge the Union Jack flutters in the wind, while on the other side the red flag with the yellow stars, being made of heavier cloth and being somewhat larger, hangs more limply.

And quite suddenly, as soon as you have crossed the bridge, you become aware of a change of atmosphere, a change of pace, a change of direction. Chinese soldiers in green uniforms were in command. We were all hurried into a palatial yellow building with large airy rooms and comfortable sofas provided with lace antimacassars, where we were counted, processed, given our instructions, and invited to take copies of Mao's little red book displayed on the shelves. Unfortunately there were no copies in English but there were quite a few in German, Hungarian, and Finnish. Then we were led through customs. There were no porters. The customs area was solid concrete—concrete floors, concrete tables, concrete ramps. Against all this whiteness our luggage looked tawdry, ill-shapen, even menacing. We were asked to make lists of our more valuable possessions—watches, cameras, tape recorders, jewelry—and warned that these objects must remain in our possession throughout the journey and would be checked when we left the country, for it was unlawful to sell them or give them away under any conditions. The customs officer had the severe expression of a man who has found no pleasure in the contemplation of human nature and suspects all foreigners of bringing contraband into his country. He searched vigorously and seemed disappointed when he found nothing.

Meanwhile our three guides had arrived from Peking, magnificently dressed in new, well-pressed Mao uniforms. Two were young women, the other was scarcely more than a boy. They told us that at each city two more guides would be attached temporarily to our group. These new guides would have the advantage of being natives of the city and would be able to answer all our questions. Our guides giggled a good deal. They were well trained, watchful, concerned with our comforts, and they continually made little speeches which they had learned by rote.

"And now we will have a little lunch," said one of the guides with a giggle.

By any standards the lunch was a feast. It was an eight-course meal held in a banqueting hall, served by an army of fourteen-year-old girls in white uniforms and dark pigtails who looked and behaved a little like marionettes, utterly expressionless. They had evidently been taught to be invisible and had almost succeeded. These exact and precise servants looked oddly alike. They had the same broad Cantonese features, the same narrow shoulders, the same quick marching walk. They were a little frightening. Even the faintest of fleeting smiles on those impassive faces would have been rewarding.

The banquet was a foretaste of many banquets to come: the huge steaming dishes followed one another in proper order; chopsticks were manipulated courageously; the snow-white tablecloth was littered with debris until it resembled a battlefield; and we staggered from the table with some difficulty, knowing that it would be quite unnecessary to eat for another forty-eight hours although there would probably be another banquet in the evening. Swollen, we advanced along a corridor to reclaim our luggage, and it was there, in the corridor, that we saw the first of the large posters which were to haunt us throughout the journey. We saw a huge blood-red fist descending on four cockroaches with human faces. The cockroaches' names were spelled out: Chiang Ching (Chairman Mao's widow), Wang Hung-wen, Yao Wen-yuan, Chang Chun-chiao, all of whom had been important members of the government and were now under arrest. Beside the blood-red fist was the inscription DOWN WITH THE GANG OF FOUR.

The poster was designed to shock by its very violence, for the fist came down like a jackhammer and the bodies of the cockroaches were so bent and twisted that it was inconceivable that they would survive. During the following weeks we would see hundreds of thousands of such posters on all the billboards of China, but this was the most powerful and dramatic of all. It was also the simplest and most accomplished, and while its ancestry could be traced to a famous Soviet poster produced in World War II, showing the red fist descending on Adolf Hitler and his armed minions, it was nevertheless colored with a peculiarly Chinese violence. It was not pleasant and not intended to be pleasant. It was an explosive call to action, clearly implicating not only the four people who were under arrest but also their followers. The main enemy was Chiang Ching, who was shown with protruding teeth and horn-rimmed spectacles, a grotesque caricature, more insectlike than the others. We would learn later that there was a good deal of substance in the charge that she had attempted to seize power after her husband's death and that she had caused untold damage by interfering in everyone's affairs, by appointing herself chief censor, and by arresting and punishing everyone who displeased her.

Inside the Blue Train all the furnishings were white—white lace curtains, white antimacassars, white seats. The landscape shone with the glow of autumn, every inch of the earth being cultivated: the banana trees had glossy leaves, the Indian corn was eight feet tall. This was another earthly paradise, like the New Territories, but more orderly and more tranquil, and strangely there were few farmers working in the fields. Pigtailed girls in black coats and blue trousers came through the train and poured boiling water into our small flowered teacups. Palm trees flashed past, and small straw-roofed hamlets, and sometimes a solitary farm cart could be seen on a lonely road. In the distance the low, wavelike hills of Kwangtung looked down on a fruitful land where there were scarcely any people at all.

In Canton railroad station there were thousands of people milling around, and there once again, written on a banner spread across an entire wall, in gold letters on red silk, was the message which I found so appealing and so mysterious:

LONG LIVE THE GREAT UNITY OF THE PEOPLE OF THE WORLD.

CANTON

The Young Mao Tse-tung

We call it Canton, but the Cantonese have other words for it. On the map it is called Kwangchow. It is also called Goat City, Fairy Goat City, Stone Goat City, Fairy City, and a few other names. According to the legend there was a time long ago when the people of Kwangchow were starving and suddenly they saw five fairies riding on celestial goats and bearing baskets of seed-grain. The fairies and the goats descended to earth, offered them the grain, and then vanished into the sky. It is a pleasant legend, and I find it easier to believe than many other legends told about Chinese cities.

None of the many names of the city sounds in the least like Canton, which is presumably the invention of a careless English scribe in the early days of the East India Company who knew that it was the capital of the province of Kwangtung and thought the capital was named after the province. The Chinese Communists have adopted a new system of romanization and they call the city Guangzhou. This sounds like a mythological beast and goes a long way to prove that the new official romanization needs improving. Under whatever name, it is the largest and wealthiest city in south China.

On this November day the flowers were in full bloom and the palm trees were waving gently in the warm wind. Canton seemed to be relaxed, with no one hurrying in the streets, and the bicyclists moved at a leisurely pace. When we asked about this, we were told that the annual Trade Fair had just come to an end and the people were resting after the frenetic activity of the past few weeks. From the top of the Red Pagoda, which served as the local museum of antiquities and was built during the Sung dynasty, we looked down on the bluish-gray roofs of the city sprawling along the banks of the Pearl River with a heat-haze hanging over it. I remarked that it looked very peaceful under the haze. My companion said: "Wrong on two counts. It is not haze, it is smog. And it is the most violent city in China, the one where all the revolutions began."

So it was, but this was not the appearance it gave from the Red Pagoda, where some dusty artifacts were on show and there were pleasant balconies to give the visitor a bird's-eye view of a city where there were no large monuments to break the skyline. The chief monument, the one object that stood out, was the Pearl River bridge built in 1928 immediately after the second and most violent revolution the city has ever suffered.

The Cantonese have quite rightly come to the conclusion that the best monument is a garden or a park. There are two enormous parks, which were attended by armies of gardeners, one called the Yellow Flower Park and the other called the Red Flower Park. The first commemorates the uprising led by a revolutionary named Huang Hsing on April 27, 1911. Late in the afternoon he attacked the yamen of the viceroy of Kwangtung at the head of 130 well-armed revolutionaries, only to find that the viceroy had fled. He burned the yamen to the ground, and the fighting continued through the night and into the next day, when more revolutionaries joined them. The local troops were well-disciplined; the fighting was bitter; the revolutionaries were forced to abandon the city. Huang Hsing escaped, but two fingers of his right hand were shot off. The government forces killed forty-three revolutionaries and captured twenty-nine, who were promptly executed. Later in the year the revolutionaries succeeded in overthrowing the Manchu dynasty after an uprising that began in Wuchang and then spread over the country. A few months later a memorial mound on Yellow Flower Hill was erected in honor of the seventy-two martyrs of the Canton uprising. It was later learned that eighty-three revolutionaries had been killed, but the words *seventy-two martyrs* had already entered history. Above the mound a curious stepped pyramid surmounted by a figure of Victory was erected, and memorial pavilions, statues of all kinds, and immense stone urns serving as flowerpots were added. Today the stepped pyramid, the statue of Victory, and all the ornamental additions have gone. There is only the mound and its containing wall, which stands at the head of an enormous flight of steps.

The uprising on December 11, 1927, was much bloodier. It was organized by Heinz Neumann, a twenty-five-year-old German revolutionary who was Stalin's personal representative in China and the chief delegate of the Third International. Except for a small part in the abortive uprising in Hamburg in 1923, he had no experience of revolutionary warfare. He was a German, spoke French, Italian, and Russian but no Chinese, and was astonishingly ignorant of all matters concerning China. Nevertheless he took command, and the uprising was launched with just over three thousand armed Communists, who began to move into the center of Canton at three o'clock in the morning, and by noon they controlled the whole city. The Red Terror began. Everyone they regarded as an enemy was arrested, and throughout this day and the following day there were summary courts-martial and massive executions. The Communists held the city for two days. Then the Kuomintang army under General Li Chi-sen marched in. The White Terror began. They killed everyone they suspected of being a Communist, including many who were not Communists. To save bullets they put their prisoners on ships, roped them tightly together, and tossed them into the Pearl River. At least six thousand Communists died during the uprising. In 1937 Heinz Neumann was arrested and shot at the order of Stalin. General Li Chi-sen suffered a curious fate. Having surrendered his troops to the Chinese Communists during the closing stages of their war against the army of Chiang Kai-shek, he was made one of the six vice-chairmen of the People's Republic of China in 1949.

Although the Communists held Canton for only two days, they had shown that it was possible for them to occupy a major city with a handful of Red Guards. A report written by Neumann some months later places the blame for the failure of the uprising on the inexperience of the revolutionaries and their lack of weapons. "In all of Canton," he wrote, "we had only 29 Mausers and about 200 bombs and not a single rifle." This was certainly not true. He obviously had no business calling for an uprising. The two-day bloodbath is known in history as the Canton Commune. Here, with the help of Stalin's agent, the Chinese Communists did everything wrong.

Red Flower Park was opened in 1957 on the thirtieth

anniversary of the uprising. The park itself was laid out by gardeners and landscape artists who took advantage of every hillock and every valley; they carved out a lake where people could go boating; they built playgrounds for children and huts where old men could play Chinese chess; and they erected a pavilion with a flaring blue-tiled roof in the traditional Chinese manner over a marble tomb said to contain the remains of five thousand revolutionaries who fell in battle or were executed by the Kuomintang. The story of the Canton Commune was told on marble walls within the pavilion. Huge masses of flowers surrounded the pavilion and the marble steps leading up to it were designed to suggest a processional road. Everything about the park and the pavilion was done with exquisite taste, and as we wandered in these gardens we had the impression that we had entered a Chinese fairyland. It was easy to forget that this fairyland commemorated a bloody uprising. Just as we were leaving the park we were reminded that flowers could be put to political use. We came upon a hedge of flowers flanking a small stone stairway. On one side of the stairway chrysanthemums had been arranged to form the words *Long live Chairman Hua Kuofeng!* and on the other side they formed the words *Down with the Gang of Four!*

Mao Tse-tung took no part in the Canton Commune. In the autumn of the same year he had led a peasant uprising in eastern Hunan, which was put down with great savagery. He fled to the Chingkan Mountains, where he set about reorganizing the Chinese Communist army and developing the strategies which would ultimately bring him to victory.

No satisfactory life of Mao Tse-tung has been written chiefly because there are very few accounts of his early life and because the last years of his life remain virtually undocumented. He has a curious habit of vanishing into his own legends: there are years when he seems to be in eclipse or in hiding and his day-by-day activities can only be guessed at. Outside of China it is not generally known that in March 1926 he became for some weeks a schoolteacher in Canton. The school was established in an abandoned Confucian temple in the heart of the city. It was known as the National Peasant Movement Institute and was ostensibly an institute for the study of peasant problems. Mao Tse-tung transformed it into a school for training peasant revolutionaries in guerrilla warfare. The old Confucian temple, dating from the sixteenth century, survives and has been transformed into a museum where you can wander at leisure from one hall, one meeting place, one study to another, attempting to capture the mood of those young revolutionaries who were determined to root out feudalism from China. A Confucian temple is always a complex of temples with many shrines, offices and dormitories, not unlike a Buddhist temple. And the very beauty of these buildings with yellow-tiled roofs and the quiet gardens prevents you from reaching into the minds of the revolutionaries, just as the brilliant blue-tiled pavilion in Red Flower Park prevents you from realizing the savagery of the uprising it commemorates.

So you wander through the Confucian temple and the outbuildings, thinking that it is entirely improbable that a man living in the seventies of the twentieth century can imagine what it is like to be a member of a revolutionary movement half a century ago. Here is the great hall with the red pillars where Mao Tse-tung, standing on a podium in front of a blackboard, delivered lectures on the techniques required to overthrow the rule of the landlords. Here is Mao Tse-tung's combined office and bedroom, which is airy and spacious, with the mosquito netting folded neatly over the strings attached to the high bamboo bedposts, and his desk, which is like any other desk, under the window. Here, too, is the long dormitory where his students slept not on beds but side by side on a raised platform covered with bamboo matting. It was said that 327 students came from twenty provinces to attend these courses. They lived hard. They were given military training by Chou En-lai. Mao Tse-tung supervised the lessons in geography with the help of a large-scale map of China made out of earth with pebbles showing the outlines of the provinces. Later the students were sent back to their native provinces with instructions to raise guerrilla battalions, to train them and arm them. With more than 300 well-trained revolutionaries the Chinese Communists already possessed a fighting force.

What happened to these revolutionaries? It appears that very few of them survived. Inside one of the buildings of the Confucian temple there are about thirty blown-up photographs of students who attended these courses. The photographs are very old and fly-spotted, made with cheap cameras, and blowing them up beyond reasonable proportions has only served to wash the character from the faces. But if you step back a few feet, they come into focus again and take on form and substance. They all look thin and gaunt and deadly serious. We learn their names and the dates of their deaths, for they all died during the revolutionary battles or during the Long March. Thus Chou Fu-hai died on April 17, 1927, probably in one of the fierce skirmishes in Hunan province. He has a long face, with prominent eyes and a half-smile playing on his lips. He was obviously one of those who could be depended upon. He has no importance to history but he might have had great importance, for he was Mao Tse-tung's closest friend. "He was a man I loved," Mao Tse-tung wrote later, and he said this about no one else.

Those shadowy photographs tell us a good deal about the beginnings of the Chinese Communists. The revolution was on the march, with Mao Tse-tung and Chou En-lai already playing major roles.

In 1926 Mao Tse-tung was thirty-two years old, but looked much younger. A photograph taken in Canton during the previous year gives him an almost girlish appearance with soft brown eyes, sensual lips, and blue-black hair swept smoothly back from his forehead. It is said that when he was in danger he disguised himself as a girl, while Chou En-lai disguised himself as a foreign missionary, wearing a black beard, a white gown, and a sun helmet. Both of them lived charmed lives. Mao Tse-tung was once captured by the local gendarmerie. He was two hundred yards from their headquarters when he slipped away, ran into a field of tall grass, and succeeded in concealing himself until nightfall. He escaped by a miracle, for sometimes the gendarmes who were searching for him came within a few inches of him. If he had been taken to the headquarters, he would have been shot.

At thirty-two he was already an experienced revolutionary responsible for at least three small uprisings in his native province of Hunan. He already saw himself as the leader of the revolution, pitting his strength against the forces of nature and even against the ruler of the universe. In his poem "Changsha," composed in 1925, he wrote:

> *Standing alone in the chill autumn,*
> *The Chiang River flowing northward,*
> *On the shores of Orange Island,*
> *I see the ten thousand hills all crimson*
> *And the forests all stained with red.*
>
> *The immense river is a glassy green*
> *And a hundred ships are racing by.*

Eagles cleave the air,
The fish swim in the clear shallows,
In the freezing air all creatures strive for freedom.

Alone in the desolate vastness,
I ask of the boundless earth:
"Who rules the universe?"
I remember a hundred friends coming here
During the crowded, eventful years,
All of them young and upright,
Gleaming with brilliance,
True to the scholar's spirit.

I remember how vivid they were
As they gazed upon rivers and mountains:
The Chinese earth gave strength to their words,
And they regarded as dung the ancient feudal lords.

Do you remember
How in midstream we struck out at the water
And the waves stayed the speeding ships?

It is passionate poetry with himself brightly illuminated at the center of the poem. He made no effort to conceal his ambitions. The character that comes through the poetry is of a man who is absolutely audacious, in love with the legends of ancient heroes, determined to risk everything on the throw of the dice, convinced that he alone possesses the power to bring about the revolution, and always exultant, even in defeat. It is romantic poetry of a high order written in the style of the Tang dynasty by a man who had immersed himself in the ancient legends and had read all the poets. His prose writings are full of dogma but in his poetry the dogmas vanish, he leaps free into a world of mythological heroes and recognizes himself among them, and there is a sense of battles waged on high mountains at the ends of the earth by giants wearing ancient armor and waving ancient battle flags. When he wrote his early poems he was so steeped in mythology that one might have thought he was living in an unreal world at the mercy of mythological demons. With him mythology became fact.

We wandered through Canton, visited factories and schools, sat down at interminable meetings with the chairmen of revolutionary committees, but we were still raw and learned very little. For me the abiding impression is of the yellow-tiled Confucian temple where the young Mao Tse-tung taught his students and stalked his prey. A Chinese artist has depicted him as a tall, serene figure in a long scholar's gown moving lightly over a storm-swept landscape, completely self-assured and conscious of his mission. It is not far from the truth.

The Mountain of Buddha

One day we were taken to Fushan, an industrial town ten miles from Canton across the Pearl River. The town, which has a population of 300,000, is little known in the West, though it has played an important role in Chinese history. On Chinese maps it is called Fushan Village for the reason that it was never walled, and by definition a city must be enclosed by a wall. It appears that the people of Fushan, who were ironsmiths, pottery-makers, and artists, at a very early stage decided to live without walls because they regarded themselves as a community of artisans whose work was so valuable that at a time of danger all the neighboring towns would come to their rescue. When the Chinese attempted to colonize large areas of southeast Asia, they took with them the iron cauldrons and cooking pots made in Fushan as a means of exchange.

Today Fushan is best known for its pottery figurines, which are exported all over China and all over the world.

Our Chinese guides told us we would be visiting an ancient temple. It was not, they said, a temple of any particular eminence or beauty: just a temple. The people no longer worshiped there, it had been converted into a museum, following the precept of Chairman Mao Tse-tung that all cultural objects should be preserved, and was now in the care of the revolutionary committee. These last words did not particularly surprise us, for it was evident that everything and everyone was "in the care of a revolutionary committee." It was a Taoist temple originally built in the Sung dynasty with a wonderfully vivid marble lion in the forecourt and many gnarled ginkgo trees in the surrounding gardens. Just inside the temple a long table had been set up and we were invited to sit down and listen to the report of the chairman of the revolutionary committee. Tea was served in large flowered cups and there was a plentiful supply of the rather harsh local cigarettes.

The chairman of the revolutionary committee announced that religion was the opium of the people and that the Taoist religion had never helped the Chinese people to raise themselves to the level of their feudal masters. Indeed the Taoist priests oppressed the people unmercifully, religion being one of the instruments of oppression. The priests in collusion with the feudal lords . . . And so it went on for about half an hour with some variations on the theme of religious bigotry and occasional references to the Gang of Four. Exhausted, I found myself studying the pottery figurines on the table, which consisted of three ducks and four penguins. I could not guess what they were doing there but it was certain that they were not made during a great period of artistic revival.

The temple, however, was enchanting. Huge glowering

gods, once gilded, gazed down from their high platforms with ferocious dignity, wielding wooden swords and halberds. They were the guardian gods of the inner shrine and no one could possibly be taken in by their ferocity, for they were as playful as the curled and periwigged lion in the forecourt. These guardian gods stood in ranks like soldiers of the heavenly guard; they leaned forward menacingly; they could cut off your head with their wooden swords and could just as easily put it back again with their powerful hands. It was pleasant to encounter them in the shadowy temple full of cobwebs and mildew. They were falling apart and were not long for this world.

Here, too, were wooden carvings showing the paradise promised by the gods, and it was clear that paradise was not very different from life as it is lived on the earth. There were feasts and banquets; girls sang and played on musical instruments; men sat in the shade of widespreading ginkgo trees. These gilded carvings were wonderfully spirited. The chairman of the revolutionary committee was disapproving. "People were very lazy in those days," he commented. "We do not live like that nowadays."

We were leaving the temple when we saw on the walls a set of posters remarkably unlike the posters we had seen in Canton. They were portraits of ancient dignitaries wearing long robes and strange caps, pointed delicately. There was an inscription saying that they were the fathers of Chinese thought and deserved to be studied, and they were evidently among Mao Tse-tung's favorite authors. They looked down from the walls like ghosts from another age.

Their names should be given here because they have some importance in history as the precursors of the Chinese Communists. The first was Wang An-shih (1021–1086), the great reformer who favored loans to poor peasants and attempted to change the nature of the governing bureau-cracy. He was a man of formidable accomplishment, a brilliant essayist, knowledgeable in economics and military affairs, and an astute prime minister. The second was Liu Tsung-yuan (773–819), a trenchant essayist of the Tang dynasty who attacked all forms of hypocrisy. The third was Wang Fu-chih (1619–1692), who was born at the end of the Ming dynasty and ferociously attacked the Manchu conquerors of China. He had no sympathy for Confucian-ism, had no belief in an ideal world of morality, and was famous for his materialism. "The world," he wrote, "con-sists of concrete things." The fourth was Tsao Hsueh-chin (d. about 1765), the author of the great novel *The Dream of the Red Chamber,* which the Chinese Communists sometimes regard as an attack on the feudal order, although this was probably the least of the author's preoccupations. The fifth was the philosopher Li Chih (1527–1620), who bitterly attacked Confucianism. The sixth was the Taiping emperor Hung Hsiu-chüan (1812–1864), who in the middle years of the nineteenth century proclaimed himself em-peror, revolted against the Manchus, and introduced a Communist and Christian rule in all the territories he conquered until the whole movement was finally put down with enormous bloodshed. The seventh was Dr. Sun Yat-sen (1866–1925), the founder of the revolutionary Kuo-mintang party and the man most responsible for the revolu-tion of 1911, which brought about the downfall of the Manchu dynasty.

This gallery of philosophers and revolutionaries was a reminder that Chinese communism had its roots in the ancient past, that it was not entirely indebted to Marx, Engels, Lenin, Stalin, and Mao Tse-tung, whose portraits appeared in so many rooms. These worthies were the seven pillars of wisdom who upheld the Chinese Communist cause, and it was right and proper that they should look down benignly from the walls of an ancient temple.

We were taken to one of the largest potteries in the world, exporting thousands of figurines every day. We watched the designers at work, the girls pouring the soft brown clay into plaster of Paris molds, the painting and the firing of the figurines in furnaces at temperatures so high that you would have thought nothing could have survived in them. It was all done quietly and methodically, to soft music and the reading of Mao Tse-tung's works over the intercom. The factory had been founded in 1952 shortly after the Communist takeover. On the same site there had been potteries for hundreds of years, and throughout all this time the method had remained unchanged except for one comparatively recent improvement: the furnaces were electrically controlled.

I had long ago hoped to see a Chinese pottery in operation, because some of the world's supreme creations have been made in them. Out of painted clay the Chinese produced their apple-green Sung bowls of marvelous delicacy, the ox-blood vases where the deep purple-red glows like the embers of a perpetual fire, and Tang horses in all the colors of the rainbow. But it must be confessed that there were no supreme creations in the Fushan pottery. The technical achievement was high. The potters could produce fantastically complicated figures three feet high, but they were rarely worth a second glance. They produced dancing girls, heroic warriors, innumerable miniature giant pandas, and busts of Mao Tse-tung. Commercialism was rampant. Imagination had gone to seed.

A visit to a nearby paper-cutting factory was more rewarding. Here young people were employed to make cutouts, cutting through twenty-five layers of colored paper to produce landscapes of astonishing delicacy. With shapes formed out of thin threads of paper these young artists were able to convey whirling dancers or armies on the march. Paper-cutting has a long history and is at least fifteen hundred years old. "Before liberation," we were told, "the Fushan paper-cutters produced golden flowers and similar things for the superstitious." But in fact they were still making golden flowers. They cut through bronze and silver foil and through twenty different kinds of colored paper. The tip of a razor-sharp knife became a paintbrush. Of necessity these artists had to work with intense concentration, and as we walked among them they seemed to be oblivious of our existence, lost in a world of their own. Their hands never trembled and their eyes never moved from the paper.

Fushan was a quiet town, lacking the hectic pace of Canton. The pottery was set in a pine forest, the paper-cutting factory in an old temple, a Taoist temple in a vast garden. The days when Fushan was famous for its forges and for the cast-iron cooking pots exported all over southeast Asia were over. A European visitor in the eighteenth century wrote that it was the most densely populated town in the world, with a population of one million. Fushan means "Mountain of Buddha" and it may have been one of the first places to welcome Buddhist missionaries. It has ample claims on history but I have never read a history of China which so much as mentioned it.

Fushan of the Forges, Mountain of Buddha, with its quiet sycamore-shaded streets and pleasant hills was a place to be remembered. It was good to be there on that cloudless day when there was only a faint nip of winter in the air and everything looked fresh and clear.

The Bicyclists

We have been told on excellent authority that in all of China from Tibet to the Yellow Sea there is not one single privately owned automobile. "Didn't Chairman Mao Tse-tung own an automobile?" we asked, and there came the immediate retort: "Of course not, it belonged to the state." "But he employed a chauffeur?" "No, the state employed the chauffeur!" So it went on. It appeared that the state owned everything except bicycles, which were manu-factured and sold by the state. Bicycles were the only luxuries that could be bought and privately possessed. "But what about television sets and radios?" "There are no tele-vision sets in private possession," we were told. "They belong to factories, government offices, government digni-taries who use them for their official purposes." "And what about telephones?" "The same."

There were no privately owned automobiles but there were at least a hundred million bicycles. They cost between $80 and $140, and for a worker who makes $30 a month they represent a large capital investment. There are park-ing lots where a thousand bicycles stand or lean together, and it is difficult to understand how a man ever discovers his own bicycle. There was a bicycle stand outside the hotel in Canton which stretched for two city blocks, an old woman guarded them, but we never saw her moving along the line to see that no one stole a bicycle. "Under socialism there is no stealing," our guides informed us. In the hotels we left the doors unlocked and felt completely safe from thieves. It must be the one country in the world where theft is rare. "And crime?" we asked. "No crime," the guides answered. "What about crimes of passion?" we asked, and were told firmly that they were unthinkable because passion was not permitted by the government.

We were fascinated by the bicycles. In the early morning and again in the evening there were a million bicycles moving through the streets of Canton. Bicycles provided the motive power for the Chinese workman to get to work and back home again. They were utilitarian, not to be used for pleasure. We never saw a boy riding a bicycle with a girl riding behind him or on the crossbar in front of him, and there was no basket attached to the handlebar large enough to hold a baby. We never saw a bicycle with lights or reflectors, and we never saw an accident. There were no three-wheelers, no tandems, no racing models, no high handlebars. Though all the bicycles were equipped with bells, we never heard anyone ringing his bell.

And in the evening, after an excursion into the countryside, we would return to the city in a Toyota bus along empty streets, and suddenly in the darkness we would be confronted by an army of bicyclists a thousand strong riding eight abreast in perfect order, all going in the same direction, all looking exactly alike, without lights, like an army of huge black moths spectral and terrifying in their silence. And in every city it was the same: the nightly invasions of the black moths.

Chiang Ching

For me especially there was a strangeness in this journey through China, for the whole country was involved simultaneously in grief-stricken adoration for Mao Tse-tung and violent hatred for Chiang Ching, and I had met both of them. In every street there were large colored portraits of Mao Tse-tung, and on every wall there were venomous caricatures of Chiang Ching. Mao Tse-tung appeared as the saving hero, huge and majestic against the sky, or in the place of honor in every room. He had become an icon. Chiang Ching, on the contrary, was reduced in these caricatures to a poisonous insect, breathing fire and filth, enmeshed in her own coils. On the one side pure adoration, on the other side undiluted hatred. They had not looked like that when I knew them.

I remembered them as people who seemed to be reasonably happy together, well-mannered, rather quiet, immersed in their work, happy with their two young daughters, one about five years old, the other about three years old. At a time when a Hawaiian-American colonel and I were the only foreigners in Yenan, they came to the showing of an American film in one of the larger caves cut out of the loess hills. The film was *A Walk in the Sun*, about a handful of Americans fighting behind the lines in Italy. It was a subject which could be expected to interest Mao Tse-tung, but the film was so episodic and the episodes were so badly put together that he became completely puzzled by it and afterward asked the colonel: "Do Americans really fight like that?" The children fidgeted and had to be quieted, and from time to time Chiang Ching would lean over them and explain what the film was all about, or what she thought it was about, for she knew very little English and the dialogue of course was in English. Mao Tse-tung had learned a little English, and though he was evidently puzzled by the drift of the film, the full-breasted Italian girls who from time to time consorted with the GIs and did errands for them, and the endless wanderings through an entirely imaginary Italian landscape, I think he was able to follow a good deal of it, for he smiled at some of the jokes and leaned forward during the rare battle scenes.

In those days Mao Tse-tung was already a legend, but he was a legend with human proportions, and Chu Teh, the commander in chief of the Red Army, was at least as legendary. In a brown uniform two sizes too large for him Mao Tse-tung was sitting in an overstuffed armchair twenty feet from a small portable screen. There were only eight or nine people watching the film—the Chairman, his wife, the two children, a solitary guard, the colonel, myself, and one or two others who had drifted into the cave. In this situation the legendary Mao Tse-tung vanished. He was like a cinemagoer in America who has heard that a film is being shown down the street, and drops in to see it.

Chiang Ching was well dressed in slacks; she had a trim body and a quiet, pleasantly musical voice; she was undeniably prettier than the other women in Yenan. It was rumored that she had been married two or three times and had been the mistress of many men before she came to Yenan. She was direct and unassuming, said very little, and looked in every way like a sensible, fond wife and the fond mother of her children.

I met her again a few days later when Mao Tse-tung gave a dinner party for one of his favorite professors who had flown up from Peking. The dinner party was attended by Chu Teh and by General Peng Te-huai, who later commanded the Chinese army that fought against the Americans in Korea. The American colonel and I were also invited. I remember that Chiang Ching spoke a good deal, but nearly always in questions, asking about everyone's health; if things were going well her face lit up, and if badly she would commiserate with the person who was suffering. Chu Teh had recently become lame, and it was believed that his lameness had something to do with the water. He was being treated by Dr. George Hatem, but there was no improvement. In his growling, gravelly voice he complained against the misery of lameness but she quickly put him at ease. At intervals throughout the dinner her voice came like a faint and pleasant tinkling.

Thirty years later the woman I remembered as gentle,

quiet and nearly beautiful was being depicted in caricatures on every wall of China, vilified and calumniated, despised and ridiculed. A massive propaganda machine had been set in motion to destroy her by holding her up to contempt. She was described as an adventuress, a traitor, a would-be empress, a deviationist, a spy, a prostitute, a taker of bribes, a buffoon, a power-mad anarchist, the poisonous worm that had somehow been permitted to enter the body politic and to exert a demonic influence. There was no vice she had not committed, no evil she had not protected. Never in Chinese history had there been such a massive and coordinated attack on a single person on such a scale. In theory the attack was directed against the Gang of Four, but the main thrust was directed at her as their acknowledged leader, the chief culprit, the instigator of a long series of criminal acts. Implicit in the denunciations was the concept of a woman so villainous that she deserved to be wiped off the face of the earth.

My first reaction in Canton was that the entire propaganda ministry had taken leave of its senses. It was inconceivable to me that Chiang Ching could have committed all these crimes or that anything could be gained by those vulgar caricatures which showed her lying in bed in various attitudes of undress, flaunting herself before television cameras, or sitting on a throne with a tottering crown on her head, frog-faced, bespectacled, and obscene. She was already under arrest. What purpose was served by endlessly vilifying her? Surely the fierce venom of the campaign was self-defeating! Such a campaign could be understood only if she was still active and dangerous, still capable of violence. Historically there was only one campaign that could be compared to it, and this took place in the pages of Julius Streicher's newspaper *Der Stürmer*, with its ferocious attacks on Jews accompanied by ferocious caricatures. Something had gone terribly wrong.

Although these caricatures appeared to represent the recent past, they harked back to the curiously named Great Proletarian Cultural Revolution of ten years earlier. It was not a revolution; it was anti-cultural; it was not exclusively proletarian; it was not great. Nevertheless it was an upheaval that profoundly influenced the course of Chinese history, and Chiang Ching played a prominent part in it. Mao Tse-tung sent the Red Guards to terrify the bureaucrats, while Chiang Ching was given special powers to restore revolutionary significance to the ballet, drama, and films. The hard Yenan line was to be maintained: there could be no ballet, no drama, no film that was not dogmatically correct to the ultimate degree. Unhappily Chiang Ching was appointed, or appointed herself, chief censor. The Great Proletarian Cultural Revolution gave a severe shaking to the bureaucracy and the arts. While the bureaucracy quickly regrouped and remained as formidable as ever, the arts suffered so severely from her censorship that they never recovered. In these strange livid posters there could be detected the pent-up anguish of a lost generation which had seen its hopes unfulfilled and had found in Chiang Ching a scapegoat, as though she alone—for she dominated every poster where she appeared—had single-handedly deflected the current of history and laid a curse on China.

Since every street in China was covered with these posters, there was not the least doubt that the campaign to discredit her had originated on the highest levels of government. A huge propaganda machine was set in motion. The cost was enormous: vast quantities of paper were being consumed, and presumably the artists had to be paid, even though they were excruciatingly bad artists. There was no wit, no grace, in these cartoons. Although hundreds and perhaps thousands of artists were employed, all these cartoons looked as though they had been painted by the same hand. Quite obviously the central propaganda bureau had issued sets of instructions, telling the artists exactly how Chiang Ching should be depicted, what words should be shown ballooning from her mouth, and what actions she should or should not perform. She always wore a skirt: a sign of capitalist decadence in a country where women wore trousers. She always wore a crown or one of those mortarboards with hanging jade beads worn by emperors. She always wore spectacles, and she was always shown with prominent teeth. She was physically repulsive. Seeing her in these posters, it was difficult to understand how Mao Tse-tung could have married her and accepted her as his wife for more than thirty-five years.

At the time of the Great Proletarian Cultural Revolution, when the Red Guards were let loose on China, it often happened that people were snatched from their beds, taken to the Red Guard headquarters, cross-examined, beaten, and then placed in a cart with a dunce's cap on their heads and their crimes written out on a white sheet tied round their bodies. Then the cart was dragged through the streets and there might or might not be a summary trial followed by an execution. The real punishment lay in the humiliation of the victim: the total loss of face. In effect, what was happening now was that Chiang Ching was being dragged in effigy through all the streets of China.

Public humiliation is a dangerous weapon because its effects are sometimes incalculable. It destroys the humiliator as well as the victim. Out of the act of humiliation flow powerful poisons. It is better, says the Talmud, to throw oneself into a burning furnace than to humiliate a human being publicly. These posters were acts of destruction: each was another bullet fired into a bullet-riddled corpse.

I know nothing to be said in her favor. I believe it is

true that she acted stupidly and dangerously. She stifled the arts of China. She possessed vast power and misused it. There is little doubt that she made innumerable enemies and had not the wit to see at the time of Mao Tse-tung's death that she was immensely vulnerable and had only one course open to her: to go into retirement as gracefully as possible like Nadezhda Krupskaya, the widow of Lenin. Instead she either made a bid for supreme power or attempted to place herself in a position where she would be able to dictate her choice to the party. Before she could deploy her strength, the army stepped in and arrested her.

I suspect that history will not find Chiang Ching very interesting as a person, but the phenomenon of Chiang Ching may be discussed for centuries. The empress Wu of the Tang dynasty and the dowager empress Tzu Hsi, who died in 1908, have something in common with her. They were usurpers without any right to the throne, but once they were in power they were utterly ruthless and vengeful, and created all manner of mischief. They were like children who enjoy tearing off the wings of flies, and it seems never to have occurred to them that they had more important tasks than destroying everything that got in their way.

What do we know about Chiang Ching? Not too much, and not too little. She was born in 1912 in a village near Tsingtao, the daughter of a small farmer who died when she was very young. Her original name was Luan Shu-meng. Adopted by a family called Li, she acquired the name Li Yun-ho, the last words meaning "white crane in the clouds." She studied in the primary school in Tsinan, joined a theatrical troupe, studied in a local drama school, abandoned acting, became an assistant librarian at Tsingtao University, and since she knew nothing at all about the workings of libraries this probably meant that she was employed in the library to fetch books and newspapers, exactly the same job that Mao Tse-tung once held in Peking University. Here she adopted a new name, calling herself Li Ching-yun, the last words meaning "blue cloud." Tsingtao University at this time was one of the major universities in China, with the poet Wen Yi-tuo, the novelist Lao She, and the short-story-writer Shen Tseng-wen on its staff. It was a time of intense intellectual activity. In the university library Li Ching-yun appeared to be settling down to acquire an education.

In 1934, when she was still working in the library, there occurred the accidental meeting that would change her whole life. A movie director from Shanghai visited the university, saw her, and suggested that she should go to Shanghai to try out for a part in his forthcoming movie. She became a player of bit parts, married a scriptwriter, and changed her name to Lan Ping, which means "blue duckweeds." In 1936 she landed her only major role, playing a shrew in the film *Wang Lao Wu*, in which she made the lives of everyone around her intolerable. Although the film was mediocre, she could henceforth say that she had been a leading actress. When the Japanese invaded Shanghai in 1937 she fled into the interior, worked for a while in the studios of the Nanking government, and in 1939 made her way to Yenan, where she became a student at the Lu Hsün Academy. When Mao Tse-tung came to address the students of the academy, she sat in the front row wearing her most fetching clothes and applauding enthusiastically. They were soon lovers, although Mao Tse-tung's second wife, Ho Tzu-chen, was alive. She was in ill-health from wounds suffered during the Long March, but she had recently given him a daughter. The politburo objected violently to Mao Tse-tung's liaison with the actress. He was forty-six, she was twenty-seven. Ho

Tzu-chen was a veteran Communist, an organizer, a school-teacher beloved by the people, while Lan Ping was raw and untrained, obviously an adventuress. A committee was set up with the task of advising Mao Tse-tung against the liaison. He thundered at them that it was none of their business and if they insisted, he would return to Hunan and become a farmer. They were in such awe of him that they relented, only demanding a promise that Lan Ping would never play any role in politics. This promise was given to them, and Ho Tzu-chen went to the Soviet Union for treatment of her wounds.

By this time Lan Ping had acquired still another name. She called herself Chiang Ching, meaning "blue river." It was said that she derived the name from a poem by Chien Chi, who lived during the Tang dynasty:

> *The song is fading, no one can be seen:*
> *Beyond the river the distant mountains are blue.*

In fact, Chiang Ching kept her promise for nearly a quarter of a century. In 1963 she fell seriously ill and when she recovered she realized she had lost her good looks. Mao Tse-tung no longer slept with her. She asked for and received permission to study the theater and to advise on theatrical affairs, concentrating her efforts on what to destroy and what to preserve. When the playwright Wu Han wrote a play called *Hui Jui Dismissed from Office* about a minister of the Ming dynasty punished by the emperor for his honest criticism, she regarded it as an attack on Mao Tse-tung, who had recently dismissed Peng Te-huai from his post of minister of defense. An obscure Shanghai writer, Yao Wen-yuan, was employed by Chiang Ching to write a blistering attack on Wu Han and his play. Yao's article was published in November 1965.

It was the trumpet blast that announced the beginning of the movement that came to be called the Great Proletarian Cultural Revolution.

Thereafter there were mass arrests, the Red Guards took to the streets, Chiang Ching became the ultimate arbiter of all matters connected with art and literature, and the seventy-two-year-old Mao Tse-tung fell increasingly under her sway. In Shanghai especially the power of Chiang Ching and her lieutenants was felt. Her chief lieutenants were Chang Chun-chiao, mayor of Shanghai, and Wang Hung-wen, a young Shanghai textile worker who had made a spectacular rise to power. Chiang Ching, Yao, Chang, and Wang continued to wield extraordinary power until Mao Tse-tung's death. Then they were arrested and the small group that had dominated Chinese politics for so long became known as the Gang of Four.

It was a strange story, and like so much that has happened in Chinese history it was almost incomprehensible to foreigners. Many intrigues and counter-intrigues were involved. It appears that all four were people of straw who acquired high positions by subterfuges of various kinds, subterfuges which would not have been possible in a more open society. Chang Chun-chiao had been a spy for the Kuomintang in the thirties; he had sent many Communists to their deaths. He was a man of great cunning and vindictiveness, and when he became mayor of Shanghai, he took pleasure in sending thousands of students to Heilungkiang and other distant regions. He detested students. He was a law to himself. He was one of those who love power for its own sake and was prepared to go to any extreme to retain his power.

The phenomenon of Chiang Ching will become clearer when more documents are published. What is certain is that she used her influence to serve her own purposes and not the purposes of China. She seemed, when I met her in Yenan, rather wistful and frail. No one could have guessed that she would emerge as a powerful figure in Chinese politics.

The Missionary

She was a small, thin, sprightly European woman with a small bun on the top of her head and she wore enormous silver-framed spectacles behind which startling blue eyes darted and flickered. She must have been about sixty, but she walked vigorously like someone half her age and she spoke very quickly and excitedly. She wore a Mao jacket and padded trousers wrinkled like an elephant's hide, and in all her movements there was a strange jerkiness. She pounced on us while we were walking through the streets of Canton, and there was no escaping from her.

"I knew you were English or American the moment I set eyes on you," she said in her high-pitched voice. "No doubt about it—the way you walk, I suppose, as though you owned the earth. So you have come to China. How gratifying for you! You have been very honored to be allowed to come here!"

We could not make her out—the accent was German or Austrian, the English was impeccably grammatical, the sharp features in agreement with the sharpness of her voice. We could not decide whether she was attempting to be accommodating or had seized upon us in order to practice her English.

"Of course," she went on, "we welcome visitors. We want them to know what we are doing. You see, we are so anxious for people to know us and not to have false impressions. We are living through the greatest experiment of all time. This country, China, is the crucible. Under the direction of our great leader and teacher Mao Tse-tung, we have drawn up the blueprints of the future. A new society is coming into being. It is my personal opinion that Mao Tse-tung is much greater than Marx or Engels or Lenin, because he has actually brought the new society into existence, and though he is indebted to the great revolutionaries of the past, he is the only one who has really brought about a Communist society, here, on this earth, in our lifetime. An extraordinary, an absolutely world-shaking event has taken place. You can see it all around you. There are no rich, no poor. Everyone is equal. No one receives special priviliges. Really, you are entering a Socialist paradise!"

Perhaps; but we were not yet sure of ourselves, for we had been in Canton for no more than twenty-four hours and were puzzled by the fact that she knew we were newcomers. She asked questions about us: where had we come from? where were we going? and when we answered, she nodded in a way that suggested she already knew the answers, and this also surprised us. When we asked her where she came from and what she was doing, she replied very quickly that she had spent most of her adult life in China, that it was the country she loved above all others, and that she hoped to spend the remainder of her days in Canton.

"It's a wonderful city," she said. "You could say it is the most revolutionary city in all of China—truly proletarian, truly Communist. Canton is the soul of the revolution. You will find other cities which are not so deeply imbued with revolutionary feeling or so loyal to our great teacher. Here, in Canton, our loyalty is absolute. You see, the Chinese Communist movement really began here, it has its roots here, it spread all over China from here, and even today it wears the marks of its Cantonese beginnings."

We were three Americans walking along one of the main streets of Canton, and all of us knew a little about the history of the Chinese Communist party. We all thought it had begun in Shanghai and that Mao Tse-tung's early achievements had been centered among the peasants of Hunan, and in fact the party was founded in Shanghai and Mao Tse-tung achieved his early fame in Hunan, but we learned later that she was perfectly accurate when she spoke of the importance of Canton in Chinese revolutionary history. Canton was the springboard, with the bloody uprising of 1927 to prove it. Here the Chinese Communists had hoped to bring about a purely proletarian revolution; it failed; the peasants had not yet been harnessed to the revolution, and it was significant that Mao Tse-tung took no part in the Canton uprising. The revolution had not, as she said, "spread all over China from here," but Canton had always been a reservoir of power for the revolutionaries, and she was right to emphasize its importance. Meanwhile she strode beside us, plying us with information we did not want, or were not yet ready for, and we were a little afraid of her and wondered how long she would dog our footsteps. Shrill, cantankerous, absolutely certain that she was living in a workers' paradise, she spoke about Mao Tse-tung as though he were still alive, as though he were a presence quite close to her, and on her sharp-featured face there glowed the light of revelation. And while she was talking about the happiness of her paradise, I remembered a missionary I once encountered in Kweichow, an elderly woman who might have been her sister, with a lined and angular face, like old leather, with a bun perched on top of her head, who glowed with the light of her Christian faith but whose lips were twisted with contempt for the Chinese who rejected her claim that she alone knew the truth, and so she consigned them to hell. I wondered why she had chosen to remain in

China at all until I realized that it was very simple: she gloried in being the one Christian in a heathen province.

During the following days we remembered the thin, sprightly woman because she was so vivid and angular and perhaps terribly lonely. She stands out in my imagination because there was something about her of the scarecrow John the Baptist who knows that heaven is within reach but is not himself really a part of it. Sometimes, too, I remember the exact tone in which she said: "You have been very honored to be allowed to come here," and it chills my blood.

The Giant Pandas

I do not know how the idea came to us, but very soon after we arrived in Canton it occurred to us that we could not leave the city until we had seen the zoo, which had the reputation of being the greatest in all of Asia. Our guides thought the request chimerical. They were stern and unyielding. There were important things for us to see; there was very little time; it was not, alas, included in the itinerary. We were told that it would be absolutely impossible to see the zoo, which was far away and had no political significance whatsoever. The zoo, it appeared, was Old China; we had come to see the New China. The request was dismissed out of hand.

In those days we had not yet learned the habits of obedience, and so we pestered the guides to telephone Peking to request a special dispensation to permit us to see the zoo, however briefly. We were being taken to one factory after another, we were being politically indoctrinated hour after hour, and within forty-eight hours of arriving in Canton, we were already suffering from the ceaseless repetition of jargon, and we wanted a holiday.

"Why the zoo?" the guides asked incredulously. "Do you really think you will learn anything from the zoo? You have come here to study—not to talk to the monkeys!"

"We have come to see China," we argued, "and the Canton zoo is an important part of China."

"On the contrary it is a very unimportant part, and we cannot waste time taking you there. We have so many important places to see. To ask for the zoo is to be very frivolous, and there is no place in Communist society for frivolity. So please don't ask us again."

But we did ask them again and again, and they finally relented, having telephoned Peking for the requisite dispensation. It occurred to them that the real reason why we wanted to see the zoo was because it contains two enormous and lively giant pandas, and they announced that we would have time to see the pandas and very little else.

The zoo was in a pleasant park to the east of the city. There was more park than zoo, the trees still green in November, and the blue lakes reflecting the dazzling blue of the sky. In Canton the houses except for the hotels, some restaurants and the gigantic Trade Fair Center have a run-down appearance, and it is obvious that no one is concerned with replastering and repainting. But the zoo was being kept in perfect order, the trees pruned, the paths swept clean, and suddenly we were aware of something totally absent from the streets of Canton. The zoo set in the lovely park had about it a sense of luxury, graciousness, and peace. No loudspeakers were playing martial music or reciting passages from the little red book. It was very quiet, very beautiful. We could very easily imagine ourselves in a China which had never known any revolutionary turmoil. Children in colorful costumes were wandering through the park. Here five-year-old girls wore bright embroidered coats, heavy necklaces, and red stockings; and their faces were painted with rouge and their eyebrows outlined with black paint. It was astonishing, this sudden emergence of the age-old China, the children running about in their finery, the laughter, the giggles, the sense of freedom. There was a time when Canton was largely ruled by foreigners who lived on the island of Shameen, flaunting their wealth and their power. That time had mercifully passed, but here and there in the city we could detect the influence of the foreign powers in the design of old buildings and street names written in English. So, too, in this park which came to resemble an ancient Chinese painting we were sometimes startled by words in English—TO THE LIONS. BOOKING OFFICE FOR ICE-CREAM. PLEASE DO NOT FEED THE ANIMALS. The booking office for ice cream was merely an ice-cream shop huddled under some ginkgo trees, with a candy store and a restaurant nearby, and there was even a kiosk with large photographs of the pandas which were not for sale, though it was possible to buy small photographs a little larger than a fingernail. These photographs were being sold at a cost of five fen each, corresponding to about two cents.

If it had been permitted, we would have stayed in the park for hours. We were dizzy with our newfound freedom as we wandered along the pathways where there were no slogans painted on the walls, no huge photographs of Mao Tse-tung, and in fact no propaganda at all. Opposite the booking office for ice cream there was a large silvery lake shaded by willows, and in the center of the lake there was an artificial island where white cranes walked in their stately fashion and a blue peacock sat in the sand with her tail outspread under the palmettos, while gray herons paraded along the shore of the island, flaunting their beauty.

This, then, was the zoo—the islands, the birds, the Mandarin ducks swimming leisurely in the lakes, and the occasional clumps of cages set at random in the parkland, a black lynx pacing between his narrow walls, a huge tawny lion—the largest I have ever seen—blinking in the sunlight. The men who designed the zoo were concerned only to give pleasure. There was no crowding of cages, which appeared to be set down at random by a deliberate effort of the designer's will. Here a set of six cages, and for half a mile there might not be another cage in sight. In this way they contrived a landscape that was wholly beautiful and intellectually satisfying, and the more we wandered through it, the more we seemed to be wandering through a Chinese painting made all the more entrancing by the prospect of coming upon exotic animals when we least expected them.

We found the pandas at last near a vast monkey house where ten different kinds of monkeys disported themselves among miniature mountains. They clambered along ropes, slid down ladders, leaped from crag to crag. There were purple monkeys, yellow monkeys, brown monkeys. There was no roof to the monkey house. The pandas were less fortunate. They were well and truly caged, though their cage was the size of a large house. They were sitting on a mound of bamboo, and eating their way through it. We had expected to see them acting playfully, but there was nothing in the least playful about them. There were two of them sitting together, but they were not interested in one another. They were interested only in tearing off small branches of bamboo and chewing them with a sound like thunder.

HANGCHOW

The Perfections of a Lake

I had Chinese friends who had lived in Hangchow and who said it was paradise on earth. But when they were asked to describe it, they failed miserably. There was a lake, there were mountains, there were temples. I would remind them that China was not altogether devoid of lakes, mountains, and temples, and they would say: "It cannot be described. You have to go there." During the war Hangchow was under Japanese occupation and it was impossible to go there.

For Marco Polo, Hangchow was quite simply the greatest, the largest, the most splendid city on earth, and in the center of it was the largest and most sumptuous palace on earth, much larger than the palace of Kublai Khan in Peking, for it had a thousand rooms each the size of an ordinary house. The palace was surrounded by parklands laid out with great art: gardens, orchards, woodlands, fountains, highways, stables, carriage houses, glades where the deer wandered and lakes where the people of the court paraded in decorated dragon boats. The main audience hall was supported by immense red and gold pillars, the carved ceiling was azure blue, the walls were covered with enormous paintings representing historical events. The private houses were almost as sumptuous as the palace, marvelously adorned inside and out. Marco Polo tells us that there were twelve thousand stone bridges, each bridge guarded by ten men, and ships passed under the bridges and carriages rode over them, and all the roads were paved and there were dirt tracks beside the roads for horsemen. The men who guarded the bridges also served as auxiliary firemen, and if a house was burning they would rush to it and help to put out the fire and rescue valuable objects which were taken to fireproof stone buildings dotted about the capital. The carriages were ornate and brilliantly painted, and each carriage could hold six people.

When Marco Polo reached Hangchow, the great days were over. The Sung dynasty had collapsed and a Yuan dynasty emperor, Kublai Khan, ruled over all of China. Hangchow was garrisoned by Mongolian troops and a Mongolian viceroy lived in the palace. Nevertheless life went on very much as it had done before. Marco Polo, who had become a high officer of state and was in Kublai Khan's confidence, made several visits to the city on official business and took careful notes. He observed that the people had no taste for war and were entirely pacific. They would look away whenever the Mongolian troops appeared. "They pursued their trades and handicrafts with great diligence and honesty, and they loved one another so devotedly that a whole city region might be taken for a friendly household, so friendly to one another were the men and women of the place." Almost it was as though the golden age had descended on the largest city in the world.

Strangely Marco Polo had little to say about the lake except that it was always crowded with pleasure boats and he had nothing whatever to say about one fact of overwhelming importance: Hangchow, conquered by the Mongols, was still the intellectual and artistic capital of China. Poets, philosophers, men of letters, historians, musicians, painters, sculptors, potters, all congregated in Hangchow because the atmosphere was conducive to creating works of art. They were able to work here because the wealth of the city sustained them and because the lake provided the perfect setting for their contemplations.

It was dark when we reached Hangchow. The lake had vanished. In the morning I woke up early, determined to see the lake before the shore was crowded with visitors. It was one of those perfect mornings when there are no clouds and the sky is a deep icy-blue. The sun had not yet risen over the low mountains in the east. There was no wind, and there were no boats out on the lake. A wide causeway ran out into the lake from the shore road and bent round to meet the road again. I walked along the causeway as the sun was rising. I had thought the lake would be immense but it was in fact quite small, about two miles broad, and there were only two small islands. The sun threw out golden streamers and finally emerged from behind the mountains, and then the whole lake became a bowl of gold.

At intervals along the causeway there were small, red-pillared pavilions with blue-tiled roofs that flared up, and there were benches for people who wanted to look out on the lake. The pavilions looked as though they had been freshly painted. I counted about twenty of them in the space of half a mile, but no one was sitting in them. I passed a few soldiers who were simply enjoying an early morning walk. Some posters had been set up denouncing the Gang of Four, but no one was looking at them.

The lake which had been molten gold gradually became blue again with only a broad golden streak carved by the low sun. I could see now that the mountains in the distance were curled like waves, very low on the horizon, and the beauty of the lake came partly from those mountains, which did not so much assert their presence as provide a necessary decoration. I had thought the lake would be wonderfully complex with hidden bays and inlets and strangely shaped islands but in fact it was very simple and its perfection came from its simplicity. I could understand a man falling in love with the lake and wanting to spend the rest of his life on its shores. Looking at this perfect lake you have the sensation of floating over it, of losing yourself in it, of drowning in the luxury of its pure colors and in the peace of the quiet waters. The lake was as light as a feather, and if you blew it away, you would find another lake beneath it.

I understood at last why the Chinese found it so hard to describe. Perfection lay in its simplicity, its very ordinariness. It was so perfect that if you saw it in your dreams you would not believe it.

The Machine-made Embroideries

Blown-up photographs of Marx, Engels, Lenin, and Stalin looked down from one whitewashed wall, while Mao Tse-tung looked down from another. The photographs were brightly colored, and there were silvery glints in the beards of Marx and Engels. Stalin, in the uniform of a Russian general, looked faintly avuncular. Mao Tse-tung's pink cheeks glowed as though he had spent his whole life in the open air and the famous mole on his chin had been airbrushed away. But when we looked closer, we saw they were not photographs: they were machine-made embroideries.

We sat at the long table listening to the head of the

revolutionary committee as she recited the statistics of the factory she commanded with so much decisiveness. She was evidently a woman born to command: she would have made a good head schoolmistress, a good head of a department store, even a good cabinet minister. The statistics came in an unending stream. The machine-made embroidery factory, which covered an area of 50,000 square meters, employed 1,100 workers, of which 53 percent were women. The average wage was 53 yuan, or $29, a month. All workers on retirement received 70 percent of their base salary. Women received 56 days of maternity leave on full pay. And so on. "All the workers know that they derive these benefits from the Chinese Communist party and they are grateful to Chairman Mao Tse-tung." In her most decisive manner, raising her voice a little, she denounced the Gang of Four, adding that all the workers shared her belief that the Gang consisted of people who deserved extreme punishment because they were traitors to the party and to the state. By this time these phrases had become extremely familiar. They were stereotypes which had worn thin from constant repetition. She said "the Chinese Communist party" worshipfully, as though it was God, and "the Gang of Four" with scorn, as though it was the devil.

We were not dismayed, for this was our environment, this was what our guides wanted us to hear, though we would have preferred simply to talk to the workers and enter their homes. Since this was not permitted, we allowed ourselves to be taken on conducted tours and attempted to gauge the quality of life in factories and schools. There was little joy in the factories and the school-children were invariably well disciplined. The heads of revolutionary committees were disciplinarians.

For centuries Hangchow had been a formidable exporter of embroidered silk. Here embroidery had been raised to an art. But machine-made embroidery is something else. We watched the designers reducing a colored photograph to ten thousand dots; each line of dots would be recorded on punched cards, and these cards in turn would be joined together on huge loops fed into the machines. There were at least a hundred machines in the factory all madly clattering away, while the loops of punched cards jerked convulsively. The final products were enormous sheets of silk bearing the images of Marx, Engels, Lenin, Stalin, Mao Tse-tung, and Chou En-lai, or else there were views of the lake with the red-pillared pavilions in the foreground. The views of the lake succeeded in making the lake look revolting, a feat one would have thought impossible, nor were the portraits of the political leaders convincing. Their human qualities had been airbrushed away. There were no pouches under Lenin's eyes, Mao Tse-tung looked astonishingly bland, Marx's white beard fell in delicate cascades. Something had evidently gone wrong and it was not difficult to see where the fault lay. It was the fault of the designers who were presumably under orders to turn out inoffensive designs and had obeyed their orders only too faithfully. The imagination which had been cultivated so strenuously during the Sung dynasty had withered away. The silkworms had lived in vain.

There were more factories and schools to be visited, but a few of us revolted. Instead we walked leisurely along the long willow-shaded causeway shaped like a stretched bow, knowing we might never see it again. It was an artificial causeway; the lake itself was artificial; and in its grace and beauty it was a supreme product of the human imagination.

The Temple of Yo Fei

In all of Chinese history there is scarcely any hero who can be compared with Yo Fei. He is the hero *sans pareil,* the one man who can be said to characterize the courage of the Chinese soldier. According to the legend his mother branded on his back when he was still a child the four characters *tsin chun pao kuo,* meaning "with utmost loyalty save the state." He was the dedicated soldier prepared to fight and destroy the enemy wherever he appeared. In his lifetime the enemies were everywhere, for the whole of north China had fallen to the invaders, and the Sung emperor, having retreated to Hangchow, was prepared to surrender even more territory to them. Yo Fei belonged to the party that rejected surrender; he would fight on to the very end even if it meant disobeying the commands of the emperor and the intriguers in the imperial court. He did not die in battle. After a series of brilliant campaigns against the Chins, Yo Fei was recalled to Hangchow, the imperial minister Chin Kuei sending him in a single day twelve successive gold tablets ordering him to appear at court. Yo Fei had no choice but to obey. He returned to Hangchow with his son, but instead of being treated as an honorable and victorious soldier, he was thrown into prison. There was a brief trial, he was sentenced to death and ordered to take poison. His son was also sentenced to death.

While Yo Fei was above all a soldier, he was also an eminent poet, a brilliant calligrapher, and a notable bon vivant with a formidable capacity for wine. A drawing of him survives in the form of an engraving on stone; he wears an embroidered gown with the insignia of his high rank and is shown reading a book, probably a collection of his own poems. He has a plump face with a wispy beard and mustache, and the large fleshy ears which the Chinese have always associated with wisdom. One imagines him pink-cheeked, at ease with the world. No doubt this was the mask he presented at court and among his fellow poets. There is more than enough evidence to suggest that on the battlefield, in full armor, he presented another aspect altogether—violent, ruthless, absolutely determined to sweep the enemy out of China. In his most famous poem, "Full River Red," he described himself at the age of thirty, and the last three lines of the poem were remembered vividly by the Chinese for the next seven hundred years:

> *My hair bristles in my helmet:*
> *Standing in the porch I see that the*
> *pattering rain has ceased.*
> *I raised my eyes to the skies and*
> *shouted with the vigor of my ambitions.*
> *At the age of thirty fame and brave deeds*
> *are nothing but earth and dust;*
> *Eight thousand li away lie the clouds and*
> *the moon.*
> *Do not tarry: the hair of young men grows*
> *white with empty sorrows,*
> *The shame heaped on us in the year of*
> *Ching Kung is not yet wiped away.*
> *When will the sorrows of the Emperor's*
> *subjects come to an end?*
>
> *O let us drive endless chariots through the*
> *Ho Lan Pass.*
> *Let our sweet ambitions be directed on the*
> *flesh of the Huns,*
> *While laughing we thirst for the blood of the*
> *Hsiung-nu.*
> *O let everything begin afresh.*

> *Let the rivers and mountains return to us*
> *Before we pay our respects once more to*
>   *the Emperor.*

Yo Fei wrote the poem in A.D. 1132. Seven years later he was murdered, and some forty years later he received posthumous honors, was given the title of a Prince of the Empire. A large tomb was erected for him on the edge of the lake, together with a temple which housed tablets recording the events of his life. Here, too, in the Chinese fashion, were many inscriptions carved in stone and carefully copied from his own handwriting.

Although many great poets and heroes were associated with Hangchow, it seemed to me that Yo Fei was one of those who deserved to be honored by the Chinese Communists. He breathed the spirit of pure resistance and indomitable courage. But when I asked the guide for permission to visit the temple, I was told that it was twenty miles away, it was under repair, and it was therefore impossible to visit.

"Why on earth do you want to see it?" he asked impatiently. "Yo Fei belongs to the old feudal order, which has been swept away by our great leader and teacher Mao Tse-tung. We have nothing in common with him. This afternoon we are visiting a primary school and a factory, and you will learn more from them than you will from an old tomb."

"Nevertheless I would like to see it. If it is only twenty miles away, I could hire a taxi."

"There are no taxis."

"Surely there are taxis somewhere?"

"Absolutely not. I told you it is impossible to see it. This is final."

So it was—for a few minutes. I had an obscure feeling

that the guide, who claimed to be a lifelong resident of Hangchow, was not telling the truth. What harm was there in visiting the tomb of a great Chinese hero? By chance, returning to the hotel, I discovered that taxis did exist and could be hired. A rosy-cheeked girl with long black braids telephoned the taxi service and said there would be no trouble at all. A few moments later she said that regrettably all the taxis were in use, but she looked puzzled, as though she did not quite believe it. By chance again, I found a map of Hangchow which indicated that Yo Fei's temple was not twenty miles away but within a stone's throw of the hotel. All this was very puzzling. Suddenly the temple, from being a remote and inaccessible place perched on a distant promontory overlooking the lake, was within reach. I should have known better. Within five minutes I was standing outside the temple, but it was still inaccessible. It had been taken over as a party meeting place, and no one except party members was admitted.

It stood there facing the lake, the gray tiles of the huge double roof and the red columns gleaming in the sunlight, with a triple flight of steps leading up to it. Some shops had been put up in the small space leading down to the lake, and the high walls flanking the temple were plastered with the inevitable caricatures of the Gang of Four writhing under the blows of their exemplary enemies. Soon perhaps the posters would be washed away in the winter rains; the shops were made of plaster and would crumble away. Although we were not allowed into the temple, at least we were allowed to gaze upon it and to walk around the high walls that enclosed the garden where Yo Fei was buried. I imagine that most of his relics have been carried away and even his tomb may have been leveled to the ground, for I could see no trace of it when I looked over the garden walls. Yo Fei had vanished, one more of the many victims of the Cultural Revolution. The ghost of Chin Kuei, the imperial minister who condemned him to death, would have been pleased. In the past the Chinese had made iron figures of Chin Kuei and his corrupt meddlesome wife, and set them near the tomb in the act of begging for mercy for the crime they had committed. It was permissible to strike them, to cuff them, even to spit on them. In all of China there were no other historical figures who received so much deserved abuse.

The meddlesome wife! We now had another meddlesome wife to haunt us. On the wall posters Chiang Ching was shown in ten different postures, looking ugly and venomous in all of them. She was a snake-woman with fangs. She was being crushed by rocks and being thrown off a precipice. She was being struck by whips and assailed by insects bearing her own face. She was everywhere on the walls surrounding Yo Fei's tomb. But the rage of the Chinese against her was a passing thing. Like Chin Kuei's wife she would have her page in Chinese history and it was unlikely that she would ever be forgotten, but it was also unlikely that her image would be cast in iron and abused for seven centuries.

We walked past the forbidden temple of Yo Fei to the botanical garden a mile away. It was afternoon, the light fading on the lake, the air fresh with the smell of pines. Sometimes we would catch a glimpse of the lake through the trees and marvel at its healing quietness. The lake dissipated all rages; so did the gardens displayed on the slope of a hill with clumps of strange trees set down with an exquisite refinement to produce the effect that everything had happened by the purest accident, although in fact everything was calculated to the last degree. There were ten kinds of bamboo, seven kinds of pine tree, four kinds of willow. On the brow of the hill the silver birches parted to reveal a lake which seemed to be lost in time, so small and secluded that it was possible to believe that no one had set eyes on it before. There was a pavilion nearby with red pillars and covered walks around a stone pool. For some reason it was decided that the pavilion needed more decoration. Accordingly Mao Tse-tung's poem "The Snow," reproduced in raised gold letters on a scarlet board as large as a bedsheet, hung on one of the walls. It was at least as decorative as the golden carp swimming in the mysterious dark waters of the pool.

By now the lake was growing dark and we walked back along the lakeside road where once not long ago there had been a great painted archway celebrating Yo Fei, with four words written on it: "Pure Blood Red Heart." Yo Fei's name was not mentioned, nor was it necessary to give his name. The inscription meant "pure courage and absolute integrity." Such qualities are rare enough in all ages, and it was a pity the archway had been torn down.

Outside the ancient temple the party dignitaries were gathering for still another meeting to denounce Chiang Ching.

SHAOHSING

The Black Yamen

All the way from Hangchow to Shaohsing my face was glued to the window of the bus, looking at the blue mountains. The other passengers were chattering away, immersed in their own affairs, while some of the most spectacular mountains in China were parading before us. They ran parallel to the highway in a long unbroken line on the horizon, and sometimes the river flowed at their feet and sometimes it swung away and reached close to the road we were traveling. The mountains were bright blue but as the afternoon advanced they turned gray and misty; and always, as though some special grace had been granted to them, they were superbly beautiful.

Students of Chinese art know these mountains well, for they were painted on long scrolls by the artists of the southern Sung dynasty and their works are among the supreme accomplishments of Chinese painting. Many of the originals are lost, but even the copies that survive are masterpieces. The mountains rise and fall like waves, and sometimes, even from a distance, you can see the precipitous slopes and feel the powerful thrust of the naked rock reaching to the crests. So the Sung artists painted them in all seasons, with the river flowing below, with perhaps a boat floating downstream, and there might be a hut or a man walking along a solitary road, and the small hut would be painted in to show the scale of the mountains while the man for all his domination of nature would be shown no larger than an insect. Now once again, as in the paintings, we saw a landscape where man was nearly invisible, for it was winter and there were few farmers working in the fields.

We were going to Shaohsing, thirty miles from Hangchow, a large industrial town with many claims to fame. Traditionally the people of Hangchow half despised the people of Shaohsing, and they liked to say "At Shaohsing there are mountains but no firewood; water but no fish; men but no loyalty." These cutting words date back to the Sung dynasty, and even today there is rancor between the two towns. It could hardly be otherwise: Hangchow with its lakes and springs, so well favored, praised by everyone and once an imperial capital ruling all southern China, and Shaohsing with its small dark canals and its factories belching black smoke. Inevitably Shaohsing dug in its heels and did its best to draw attention from its powerful rival. During the Sung dynasty the riffraff of Hangchow were sent there, and so there came about a tradition of rebelliousness. Shaohsing became famous for a class of people called "the beggars," who sometimes had the whole town at their mercy. Rebelliousness bred clever lawyers, revolutionaries, and malcontents who secretly pretended to be working for the government but were in fact attempting to undermine it. In the days when Sun Yat-sen was attempting to overthrow the Manchus, a young woman from Shaohsing took part in a plot to assassinate the viceroy of Anhui. Her name was Chiu Chin, and the plot was organized by her cousin, a young schoolmaster called Hsu Hsih-lin. The viceroy was shot dead while attending the commencement exercise of a police institute. Hsu Hsih-lin made no attempt to escape. He was tortured and executed, and his heart was cut out and presented to the viceroy's family. Chiu Chin was arrested shortly afterward, and on the eve of her execution she wrote a seven-word poem which became deservedly famous:

> The autumn wind and the autumn rain
> Mortally torment a man.

Until recently there was a small museum in Shaohsing in honor of Chiu Chin, the dedicated young schoolmistress who attempted to rid China of one of its Manchu overlords. Four years after her execution, in 1911, the Manchu dynasty fell in ruins.

Today Chiu Chin is nearly forgotten, and the Chinese Communists are more inclined to honor Lu Hsün, the novelist and short-story writer, who was also born in Shaohsing and whose works were regarded by Mao Tse-tung as among the greatest produced in our time. And all over China Shaohsing is remembered for something that has nothing at all to do with rebellion and literature: it is the home of Shaohsing wine, sweet and yellow and seemingly innocuous, but a man can get wildly drunk on four small cups of it.

We came to Shaohsing late in the afternoon—a seemingly shapeless town with broad unpaved streets and stone bridges over the canals, dominated by the twin steeples of a church long ago deconsecrated and a forest of factory chimneys. It seemed to have no center and no circumference. Because there was no hotel, we were taken to an old yamen set among bleak hills four or five miles beyond the town. This yamen had been taken over by the Red Army and converted into a kind of hostel. Once, under the Manchu dynasty, it had served as the headquarters of a local official who presided in the great hall under the flaring double roof; here he issued commands, received petitions, and entertained his guests. It resembled a small palace and retained a certain elegance. The rooms around the courtyard had been converted into bedrooms; the gatekeeper's lodge had become a barbershop; meals were served in the great reception room, which was very drafty.

Even now I am haunted by this dark yamen guarded by two colossal marble lions which testified to the importance of long-dead officials in flowing gowns who once ruled over this small corner of China. It was a palace gone to seed, dark, uncomfortable, and bitterly cold. We came to the yamen relatively healthy and left it like sick people, coughing and sneezing, suffering from strange chills and aches, and with little joy in life. There was no heat in the bedrooms; the bedcovers were ice-cold; the lavatories did not work. An age-old damp seemed to have settled on the place. Someone would start coughing, coughing, and then everyone would be coughing, just as a single barking dog will set all the dogs in the neighborhood barking. We went to bed fully dressed and pulled our overcoats over the bedcovers, but somehow the cold air penetrated our skins and lodged in our bones. We shivered through the longest of all the nights we spent in China.

In the clear, cold morning air the yamen was still a thing of beauty, though no flowers grew in the formal garden and no water flowed in the ornamental pools. The Red Army had quite properly taken it over and used it for its own purposes, but they had failed to make it livable for visitors. For us it was a dark and mysterious place lost among the hills, and we wished we had never been there.

Hung Shan Commune

They had taken us to the yamen, I suppose, because this was the nearest lodging to the Hung Shan commune, which lay some fifteen miles away among the rolling hills. It was said to be a model commune, well known in the province as one of the most advanced, supervised by a revolutionary committee that had satisfactorily solved many of the urgent problems facing communal life. It was set in a broad valley watered by streams from the surrounding mountains and by underground wells. In former times the entire valley had belonged to a single landlord who was cruel and avaricious. There were 85 houses in the village, and of these 70 were the hovels of poor peasants who eked out a living by gathering firewood in the hills and carrying sedan chairs. I had seen such poverty-stricken villages in Szechuan during the war and met those landlords who regarded every villager as their own private property. Now, according to the head of the revolutionary committee, there were 172 households in the village and 782 inhabitants. The land was supporting twice as many people as it did in the past, and every inch of the earth was being cultivated.

He was a man of middle age, swarthy, hard-headed, obviously capable. He was the new landlord, the man in charge, with a driving force which was apparent in his sharp gestures and abrupt voice, and he was very likable in spite of his rough manner. He was of the earth, earthy, and there was no trace in him of the deceiving bureaucrat. He was the kind of man who, if anything went wrong, would roll up his sleeves and try to solve the problem single-handedly. As we accompanied him around the commune we came to have a healthy respect for him and for his farm workers.

"One of our most notable achievements," he was saying,

"is that we have full control of the water supply. That river you see over there at the foot of the mountains was made by us. We carved the channel. We fed the water into it. We made it, and can use it in any way we please. These fields full of vegetables are watered from an underground spring which we discovered farther up the valley. We have twenty hectares of land, ninety hectares of bamboo, four hectares of tea plantations, and for all of them we need water. We have even built a reservoir. We have done everything that man can do to ensure that for generations to come the farm workers in this valley will have enough water for their needs, and more to spare."

The tea bushes seemed to be his favorite. "We pick only the tender leaves," he said, and went on to explain the workings of the twelve gleaming machines resembling pressure cookers which were housed in a shed overlooking a threshing floor. The machines, each about six feet high, did not look as though they had been built in the commune; nor were they. "We paid for them out of our own money," he said proudly. They were for drying out the liquid in the leaf and for fermenting the leaf to reduce its astringency. They were made in Canton. "Before 1958 we had to do all this work by hand," he said. "Now we have machines. We are progressing."

Some of us asked him whether progress was worthwhile, for the machines put people out of work and how can machines operate as carefully as human hands?

He looked at us incredulously.

"You use machines in America?"

"Yes."

"Well, we have a right to use them here. Listen. In the past it took twelve man-days to produce fifty kilos of tea. Today with our machines it takes one man-day to produce fifty kilos of tea. Isn't that progress?"

We said it was not necessarily progress. Automation

was not necessarily progress. Progress was a devil that had caught us by the tail.

"So you want us to abolish the machines?" he asked, looking more incredulous than ever.

"No," we said, "but perhaps after all the best tea is made by hand."

He disputed this statement: the best tea in the world came from his machines.

We walked across the threshing floor to see a small dispensary supervised by a barefoot doctor who resembled a young Buddha. He looked about sixteen, and was perhaps twenty. The health of 782 people in the commune depended on him. He was asked how he had obtained this post, and said he had trained as a barefoot doctor in Hangchow and the party had sent him there. Had he been given a choice? No, he had gone where he was told to go. Was there any place he would have preferred? He seemed puzzled. "I go wherever I can serve the people," he said. "The party tells me where to go." He said this smiling and with absolute conviction.

A little while later we were taken into the house of one of the farm workers. He was small and weather-beaten, and his skin was drawn tightly over his cheekbones. He had a quick infectious smile and great patience. That he was a farmer, had spent all his life as a farm worker, was evident from his hands, which were the color of the black earth in the fields, the thick black fingers heavily scarred. He lived in a small narrow house with three tiny rooms on the ground floor and three upstairs. The upstairs rooms were all bedrooms. His monthly rent was one yuan. He had two sons and two daughters, one of them married, and in addition there were his mother and two grandsons. Four generations were living in the narrow house and the two youngest were peering round the door, doll-faces illuminated by dark and flickering eyes.

There were four or five of us gathered round him in a bare whitewashed room with a stone floor. A table, five small stools, a calendar, a colored lithograph of the young Mao Tse-tung: nothing more. We asked him how much he earned. About 1,700 yuan a year, which is $1,000 at the prevailing rate of exchange. He said his needs were modest and he usually saved about 1,000 yuan, the money going into government bonds at 2½ percent interest. He was the careful farmer, cautious with money, purchasing only what was essential. "What can I spend money on?" he asked. "Food? The food comes from the commune or from our own little plot of land. Clothes? I cannot wear more than one suit of clothes at a time." Money was inessential; it meant nothing at all. "If you were in Peking and saw the shops, wouldn't you want to buy something?" He thought this over for a while and said: "I have a radio. I have a watch. What more is there?" He had been a farm worker all his life, was once poor, was now rich in worldly goods. He led us upstairs to the bedrooms, where the beds were so large that they filled nearly all the space. Everything was spotlessly clean. There were brassbound chests full of linen, heavy bolsters, a teapot shaped like an elephant, a picture frame containing miniature photographs of his entire family, each photograph being about half an inch square, and some straw mats. These rooms were spartan by our standards, but he was evidently satisfied with them. He had the air of a man who had acquired all he wanted to acquire and asked for nothing more. He lived for his family and the commune. Except for a single visit to Hangchow in his youth, he had never left this valley. He said he was sixty-one and looked about seventy.

We had seen many communes but this was the largest we saw in the countryside. It was well run, very calm, very orderly. The people looked well fed and the children had rosy cheeks. They were a little solemn, a little shy of the foreigners in their midst. There was no effusiveness and the speeches were mercifully short. We half envied these farmers who lived in an enchanted valley far from the cities. Later it occurred to me that something was missing: nowhere in all the houses and in all the buildings we visited did we see a single newspaper, magazine, or book.

As we were leaving, the chairman of the revolutionary committee took us to a small hill looking over the valley. The hill was thickly covered with tea bushes with small white and orange flowers hidden among the deep-green leaves.

"I have told you about the landlord who once lived here," the chairman said, standing on the top of the hill. "Well, he was a very strange man. He was very cruel, he wanted as much money from his estate as possible, and he drove his farm laborers almost out of their minds. He was also very superstitious—he was desperately afraid of storms and dragons. He really believed in dragons. He thought there was a dragon living under this hill where you are standing, and because of this nothing could ever be planted here while he owned the estate. They would tell him: 'It is good land. Why waste it?' and he would say: 'If we planted anything here, the dragon would come out.' He really believed this.

"When liberation came in 1949 we set up a revolutionary committee which was very busy organizing work in the fields. At first, of course, it was not a commune—that came later. The farm workers remembered the old landlord's talk about Dragon Hill but did nothing about it for some years. Finally they decided to plant tea here, though there were still some peasants who thought the land was cursed. Perhaps it was an old burial mound, perhaps there really was a dragon living under the hill. But the tea bushes grew and flourished, and it was the very best tea grown in the valley."

"What happened to the landlord?" someone asked.

"He ran away. I suppose he took the dragon with him."

A Memorial to Lu Hsün

We returned to Shaohsing at night when it had lost all resemblance to a town and looked like a stage setting for a play set in the Middle Ages—dirt roads, ancient buildings with curling eaves, stone bridges over somnolent canals, only a misty light coming from the rare streetlamps. There were unpaved streets that cannot have changed very much since the days in the Sung dynasty when the city councillors of Hangchow rounded up the ruffians and exiled them to Shaohsing. It was late; there was scarcely anyone in the streets; and a bitterly cold wind was blowing. On a night like this it was easy to imagine Chiu Chin slipping through the dark streets with a pistol hidden in her gown.

We walked cautiously because the ice was forming on the ground and because the road was full of potholes. At the side of the road there were ditches full of black water, and we wanted at all costs not to fall into them. The wind howled and the thin trees were waving against the cold, cloudless sky. The oldest among us hid our hands in our sleeves to keep warm and the youngest thought they could achieve the same by running about in the darkness.

At last we came to a small house that could not be distinguished from any other house in the street; it was very old, very ordinary, and very dark. There was a long passageway leading to a wild garden, where Lu Hsün had played as a child. There were heavy blackwood tables, shining pots and pans in the kitchen, and huge canopied beds. We were told that if Lu Hsün returned to life, he would recognize every table, every pot, every bed: the statement may not have been quite true, for in one of the most moving of his autobiographical short stories Lu Hsün tells us how when he was a young man the entire family was evicted from the house and all the furniture was sold or given away. From this small, gloomy house we were taken to another house five minutes' walk away. It was an old temple long ago converted into a schoolhouse. The children's desks were in place; Lu Hsün's desk was pointed out to us, and his portrait—the somewhat patrician features, the heavy mustache, the hollow eyes—gazed down from the walls. He was an author, a short-story writer, a journalist, and a poet who achieved considerable fame after the publication of his long short story "The True Story of Ah Q" in 1921. It describes the short unhappy life of a bumbling, good-hearted, bad-tempered ne'er-do-well who had the misfortune to attract the attention of a government official. There were riots in the town. Ah Q very sensibly avoided taking part in them, but he was arrested because the government official thought he was probably one of the rioters. He was therefore executed. The government derived some satisfaction from the execution, which served as an example to others. Ah Q found no satisfaction, and the people who watched the execution were annoyed because he was shot to death and not decapitated, which was always a more exciting spectacle. The story is told with controlled fury: Lu Hsün rages at all his characters, finding no redeeming characteristics in any of them. The feudal lords of the town, the government officials, the soldiers and the rioters and Ah Q himself are beyond saving. The town is obviously Shaohsing, and Ah Q is just as obviously a disguised self-portrait.

Lu Hsün, whose real name was Chou Shu-jen, was born in Shaohsing in 1881, the son of a scholar who never received any appointments and the grandson of a scholar-official who was holding office in Peking at the time of Lu

Hsün's birth. When the boy was thirteen, his grandfather was thrown into prison. Thereafter the family lived in poverty, supported by his courageous mother. His father died; he was continually being sent to the pawnshops; he knew what it was like to walk barefoot in winter. But he was a good scholar who enjoyed the ancient Chinese Classics, did well in school and was considered a suitable candidate for the Naval Academy. He passed the entrance examination, found he had no liking for the nearly non-existent Chinese navy, switched to the School of Railways and Mines, and in 1901 he graduated and was awarded a scholarship to study in Japan. Restless always, he switched again—this time to a medical school. In 1906, when he was twenty-five, he abandoned the study of medicine, saying that he no longer felt the need to cure Chinese bodies, it was more important to cure their souls. He became a writer. Then because writing is a notoriously ill-paid profession he became a schoolteacher. In 1911, when the revolution broke out, he was the principal of the Shaohsing Normal School. A few months later he became an official in the Ministry of Education in Peking.

It was a career that was all happenstance. He was continually jumping around, trying to find a direction. While serving as an official, he annotated ancient texts and made a prolonged study of the Buddhist texts translated into Chinese during the Tang dynasty. He was thirty-six years old when he published his first short story, "A Madman's Diary," a profound meditation on the theme "Is it right for one man to eat another?" The idea came from the fact, well known in Shaohsing, that Hsu Hsih-lin's heart had been torn out of his body after he was executed, and presented to the family of the Manchu official he had assassinated. Then he turned the idea upside down. Everywhere officials were eating people and quite ordinary people were eating people. In the last words of the story he wrote: "Perhaps even now there are some children who have not eaten people. Save the children. . . ."

He was a writer enraged by society, with a driving passion for justice. He was among the first who wrote in *pei-hua*, the common language of the people, but he wrote it with a scholar's grace and a scholar's deliberate calm, which made his writings all the more effective. He wrote slowly, with great care. Stories were told about how he wrote out sentences and then pasted them on the bare whitewashed walls of his room in Peking: one sentence high up on the right would be near the beginning of the story, another sentence down on the left would come toward the end, and there would be four or five sentences in the middle of the wall. In this way, by adding more sentences, he would gradually build up the story *architecturally*, assembling the building blocks in the proper order. He wrote his stories slowly and painfully, but an article for a newspaper or a magazine might be written in an hour, passionately, without pausing. One of his most famous articles was written in 1930 after learning that six young writers had been captured by the Kuomintang police, ordered to dig their own graves, and then buried alive. The executions were carried out in secret, and Lu Hsün protested bitterly against the executions and also against their secrecy:

There was a time not very long ago when a prisoner condemned to death was led through the busy highways and he was allowed to protest in the loudest voice against his condemnation, he could say the vilest things against his judges, he could tell the story of his brave deeds and demonstrate his courage in the face of death. At the moment when he was about to be executed, the spectators

The young Mao Tse-tung.

Guardian lion at Fushan.

Chiang Ching on target at kindergarten in Canton.

Chiang Ching firing broadsides. Wall poster.

The Gang of Four, as bugs and insects withering in
the sun. Chiang Ching at upper right.

Lu Hsün.

The young Mao Tse-tung.

Yenan. August 1946. Mao Tse-tung, American colonel,
Chu Teh, Peng Te-huai in back row. Chiang Ching at
lower left, author at lower right.

would applaud. When I was young, I thought the practice was barbarous and cruel. As I grow older, it seems to me that the rulers of the past were courageous and supremely confident of their power in permitting these things to happen. And perhaps it showed that the rulers were showing their kindness and even benevolence to the condemned man. But nowadays this no longer happens.

This passage comes from an article called "Written in Deep Night," published with some omissions in Shanghai in June 1936. Five months later Lu Hsün died of tuberculosis.

Lu Hsün was a good writer at a time when there were many good writers in China. Wen Yi-tuo, Hsu Chih-mo, Shen Tseng-wen, Mao Tun, Pien Chih-lin, Lao She—another ten or twenty names could be added—all wrote magnificently and accurately recorded the feelings and atmosphere of the age. All inevitably wrote works of social protest. The Chinese Communists have singled out Lu Hsün as the one writer of eminence during this period and have permitted all the others to be forgotten. In their pantheon he remains supreme, although he cannot serve as an example to Communist writers, since he vigorously attacked the society in which he lived.

Everywhere you go in China you are likely to find the works of Lu Hsün. His books were on sale in Canton; there was a special exhibition to commemorate the fortieth anniversary of his death in Hangchow; Shaohsing commemorated his death with an enormous building large enough to house an industrial exhibition. The building must have cost the equivalent of two million dollars. In the lobby you are greeted with a six-foot-high bust of the short-story writer in white plaster, with a hundred chrysanthemums growing at the foot of it. Then, in room after room, there are blown-up photographs of Lu Hsün taken during all the stages of his life. There is Lu Hsün as a baby, Lu Hsün sitting in a deck chair in his garden in Shanghai. He had an appearance of strength, delicacy and intelligence, and it is pleasant to watch him growing up. But it must be confessed that he grows up very slowly, for there are fourteen large rooms with four or five photographs in each room. The walls are sixteen feet high; even the largest blown-up photograph is dwarfed by the high walls, and you go from one room to another hoping to find something more meaningful than still another portrait of a good writer whose features are fairly well known to anyone who knows anything about modern Chinese literature. Soon we become aware that something very strange is happening. Lu Hsün is becoming deified and in the process of deification he is becoming insubstantial. The more we see of him the more he evaporates before our eyes.

About halfway through the exhibition an attempt is made to identify Lu Hsün with the emerging Chinese Communist party. He was never a party member, never sought entrance into the party, never permitted himself to lose his independence. He detested the government of Chiang Kai-shek and hoped that a better government would emerge. The Chinese Communists claim him for their own. "He was the chief commander of China's cultural revolution," wrote Mao Tse-tung. "He breached and stormed the enemy citadel. On the cultural front he was the bravest and most correct, the firmest, the most loyal and the most ardent national hero, a hero without parallel in our history." A modest man, Lu Hsün would have wondered how any man could live up to so many superlatives.

In the last room are gathered his relics—his brown shoes, his brown hat, his brown scarf, the white gown he wore in summer, his brushes and ink slabs, the last X-ray showing his diseased lungs, a letter from Madame Sun Yat-sen begging him to recover quickly, and an article he wrote two days before his death. There is a photograph of him taken a few moments after his death with the death sweat still on his brow.

Shivering in the cold wind, we left the huge white museum in the little-visited town of Shaohsing to ponder the mysteries of fame and the strange processes of deification.

NOTES FROM
A DIARY

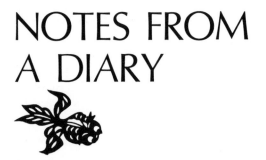

Strangely not one of us thought to bring a shortwave radio, with the result that we have not the faintest idea what is happening in the outside world. Some of us have little clock radios and I have a little battered pocket radio which faithfully records Chinese songs coming apparently from Shanghai, and nothing else. It is perfectly legal to bring in shortwave radios on condition that they are not sold or given away: all cameras, radios, phonographs, even watches are listed on a manifest made out at the port of entry, and we have been told that the manifest will be carefully scrutinized when we leave.

So we have become hungry for news. It is an almost physical hunger and we feel deprived. For us news is oxygen. It stimulates us. A constant stream of headlines feeds into our blood and without it we are in danger of losing our minds. There are not even any rumors. We have seen no Chinese reading newspapers except the very rare newspapers pasted on the walls. They read the "big-character" posters denouncing Chiang Ching, but they appear to read them listlessly, without much interest. The posters are denunciations—not news. We talk about the absence of news, we tell ourselves that reading the newspapers is a waste of time, it is a habit like smoking or taking drugs, and we learn nearly nothing. But the hunger remains.

We have brought this problem to the attention of the guides, who are not in the least sympathetic. We have never seen them reading a newspaper. They tell us that when we get to Shanghai we will be able to find the daily communiqué issued by the Chinese Communist government in three or four languages—it is just a question of waiting patiently. But we are out of patience. Surely great and important events are happening outside in the world: treaties are being signed, politicians are being assassinated, oil slicks are contaminating the oceans. The thin guide with the suspicion of a harelip gives the faintest of smiles.

"Why do you want to know?" he asks.

We explain patiently that news is our lifeblood, it is something we need like bread or rice. His smile broadens in incredulity.

"What you call news is not important," he announces.

As we are leaving he calls after us: "We Chinese have just exploded another hydrogen bomb."

"Very well," I said bravely, "we shall revolt! It is time the guides learned that we are not dormice! They are always telling us where we have to go. It is time we told them where we want to go!"

"Where do you want to go?"

"Into the houses of ordinary people, the offices of high officials, the students' dormitories, the houses of detention, the homes for unwed mothers, the restaurant kitchens! We are taken to a factory and told that it produces x million square yards every year, that the laborers are paid *x* yuan a month, and so on, and so on, and it is not on a human basis at all. We ought to be seeing more people and fewer factory bosses."

No one was paying the slightest attention.

"We are not seeing the Chinese people," I went on. "We are seeing the bureaucrats, who are the same all over the world. Why don't we just go on strike? We tell them: Let us see the Chinese people, or else—."

It occurs to me that I am making no converts and that everything will go on as before. We sit at the long tables with their patterned tablecloths while the factory boss reads out of his notebook a well-rehearsed account of the factory's achievements, while behind him in the distance, unreachable and remote, unquestioning and multitudinous, are the Chinese people whom we have not yet encountered.

What is most tragic about the China we have seen so far is that so much of it is second-rate. We have met no first-rate intelligences, although they undoubtedly exist. Conformity produces dullards, and most of the Chinese we meet play for safety by reciting the jargon appropriate for the occasion. Ironically, this is precisely what Mao Tse-tung did not want, although it became inevitable once the monolithic state was imposed on China. Once the feudal classes, the landlords, and the rich peasants had been swept away, he expected that Communist rule would weigh lightly on the people. In fact it weighs very heavily on them and there is no escape. The weight comes from the party bosses, the general poverty, the absence of incentive, and the lack of imagination. For ten years China has been standing still.

A nation needs new ideas, new objectives, new horizons. Forty years ago, when Edgar Snow came to Yenan, the Chinese Communists had new ideas in abundance, their objectives were clear, they knew where they were going. In those days Mao Tse-tung was saying that communism had nothing whatsoever to do with personalities; whether he lived or died was a matter of no consequence to the revolution, which possessed its own momentum. But as the years passed, the revolution crystallized around him and around his legend. He became the savior, the red sun in the East, the helmsman, the destined leader. Apparently he made no serious effort to escape from under the legend he deliberately fostered. When Snow asked him about this, he answered that the people needed someone to worship, it was a primitive necessity, and there was very little he could do about it, implying that it was too late to do anything about it. Hence the innumerable portraits, medallions, badges, statues, his handwriting on every billboard, and the little red book. His presence everywhere, like a gas filling up the spaces between individual lives.

Well, it was not like this in Yenan. In those days he was a man with great dignity: the legend possessed human proportions and had not escaped into those regions where it became hopelessly diffused, like the Holy Ghost. When he spoke in Yenan, no one bowed low to the ground. When he came walking into the room with Chu Teh, you saluted Chu Teh first because he was the older man. He had not reached the position of divine infallibility he occupies now. He was not worshiped and would have regarded "worship" as totally offensive, totally undesirable. In retrospect we can see that during the last ten years of his life he demanded to be worshiped. Heroic materialism was not enough; human dignity was not enough; he became a god.

Legends, even those legends which come about as the result of massive propaganda, act sometimes in unpredictable ways. They acquire a critical mass, explode, give off contrary legends, which sometimes feed upon one another, and disintegrate in order to acquire new protean shapes, new avatars. Because they are unpredictable, they are profoundly dangerous. They have a life of their own, but it is not life as we know it, for they can destroy themselves many times over and still survive, attracting new and unfamiliar legends, continually reinventing themselves. Already the heroic portrait of Mao Tse-tung, which looks down upon us wherever we go, is changing its expression. We see him in his pride and in his power, and at the same time we see him lying in his glass shell in Peking, with closed eyes and sunken jaw, withered and old and very tired as he lies with a red blanket up to his shoulders. There is very little resemblance between these two portraits.

We were told about Chiang Ching's "five falsies": false hair, false eyebrows, false teeth, false breasts, and false hips. Apparently the phrase was current long before her recent fall from power, suggesting that the battle lines may have been drawn up long ago. With these "five falsies" she is reduced from being a woman to an object, to something that scarcely exists and therefore lies beyond the reach of human sympathy.

We are told that she is in prison, under house arrest, in exile in some remote region of China, in hospital, or in a lunatic asylum. No one really knows where she is or what will happen to her except presumably the army, which arrested her. She has not yet become a "nonperson," for the caricatures on all the walls show her to be ferociously alive, and in fact these caricatures are designed to prolong her legend—the legend of the insanely inept and yet dangerous woman who may or may not have attempted to seize power after her husband's death.

After the winter rains, will they still be painting her on all the walls of China?

Romanized Chinese. Matteo Ricci, the seventeenth-century Italian Jesuit who was among the first to bring Western scientific knowledge to China, may have been the first to experiment with romanized Chinese. The Chinese themselves claim that a certain Fang I-chih reduced the Chinese characters to an alphabetic script about A.D. 1650. They have been talking about it ever since.

The trouble is of course that the beautiful Chinese characters simply do not submit to the tyranny of the roman alphabet. With a phonetic alphabet we can reproduce the sounds of Chinese fairly accurately, but our ordinary alphabet is too limited. There have been many systems of romanization, but it seems to me that the Chinese Communists have chosen the worst. Everywhere you go in modern China you will find romanized Chinese: it is written on all bank notes, on many shops, hotels, and restaurants, and at railroad stations and over the doors of some official buildings. Place-names and personal names sometimes have a very odd look indeed. Peking becomes Beijing, which is closer to the way the Pekingese pronounce the name of their city, but not close enough. Mao Tse-tung becomes Mao Ze-dong and Chou En-lai becomes Zhou En-lai. Tsingtao becomes Qingdao. Tsinan becomes Jinan. The emperor Chien Lung becomes Qian Long. The dowager empress Tzu Hsi becomes Ci Xi. There is method in this madness, but it takes a long time to grow accustomed to these *X*'s, *Z*'s, *Zh*'s, *Q*'s, and *C*'s to which new arbitrary sounds have been attached. Chinese romanization looks like strings of barbed wire. Aesthetically there is almost nothing to be said for the new romanization, but it may be too late to change it. The Chinese government has decided that this is how it will be. Chinese, in its official romanized form, looks curiously like German.

In the Yenan days they were talking about abandoning

the Chinese characters altogether because they were so difficult to learn. There are said to be about eighty thousand Chinese characters, of which about eight thousand are in current use. But how can you print a newspaper with eight thousand different characters? The Chinese Communists sensibly restricted their newspapers to two thousand characters and were able to say what they wanted to say very forcibly and without any difficulty. But even now there are people who believe the Chinese characters will have to be swept away in the interests of speedy communication and a lighter work load for students learning Chinese. There are some ominous signs. In all the schools we visited the pupils were learning romanized Chinese as well as the familar Chinese of curving strokes, dots, and splashes forming the most beautiful ideograms ever invented.

The beauty of the Chinese characters! Even when five-year-old children write it, it has character and grace. The children write boldly. This is how it should be, for they are the inheritors of a language which was not originally intended as a medium of communication between mortals. When we first come upon the Chinese characters they are being carved on the shoulderbones of sheep and goats in the form of questions addressed to the gods. The bones were then plunged into the fire and the Chinese believed that the marks of scorching and burning, and the cracks in the bones, indicated the replies of the gods. So there appears to have been a common language, a court language, and a special language reserved for communication with the gods, and it is the last of these that survived. Chinese is probably the only surviving language invented as a means of communicating with the gods.

You can tell a good deal about a country from its coins and bank notes. Chinese coins are very small and thin, and being made out of aluminum they do not weigh heavily in the pocket. They are so light that you can carry fifty of them in your pocket without being aware that you are carrying any of them. The design on the coin is stamped very thinly, so that it is difficult to recognize the great seal of the People's Republic of China. These lightweight coins, so frail, so easily bent and so easily lost, seem to be looking forward to a time when money will have vanished from the face of the earth.

Since the Chinese invented paper, you might expect them to produce a fine well-seasoned paper for their bank notes. In fact they are printed on cheap paper which is only a bit better than newsprint. The notes tend to crumple, to become shapeless masses of greenish-gray pulp. Mao Tse-tung does not appear on them. The two-yuan note, worth a little more than a dollar, shows on one side a woman on a tractor and on the other a shepherd. The five-yuan note shows a steelworker on one side, and on the other you can see a train and a power shovel. The artist has not been especially imaginative in his designs, and these easily crumpled notes are totally devoid of the mystery and grandeur of money. Which, after all, may be what they intended.

On the Train. I have read accounts of train journeys through China where loudspeakers blared out music and readings from Mao Tse-tung's little red book. A train journey became a psychedelic experience with the passengers drowned in sound and propaganda. But there is nothing at all like this during the journey from Hangchow to Shanghai. The music plays very softly. Every ten minutes or so a girl comes along to refill our teacups with hot water from a kettle. The tea is excellent; so are the furnishings on the train. The curtains are a soft, delicate blue, and there are flowering plants on the window-tables. Only one thing disturbs me: we left Hangchow at 6:30 P.M., darkness fell quickly, and we shall not see the landscape between Hangchow and Shanghai.

We observe that the Red Army soldiers on the train are already wearing their heavy fur caps. It was bitterly cold in Hangchow and it will be colder in the north.

SHANGHAI

The Cloud-capped Towers

The moment you come off the train in Shanghai you become aware of a faintly cloying smell. It is difficult to put a name to it, but it resembles the smell of burned sugar, licorice, and decaying leaves, and it pervades the whole city. No one seems to know where it comes from. It is a rather heavy smell, not unpleasant, at once sweet and acid, and once you have smelled it you never forget it. It is not the smell of the sea, for we are far from the sea. Mostly it is the smell of burned sugar, and it is present even when there is no wind.

I wondered whether I would recognize Shanghai, whether it would have anything in common with the Shanghai I knew when it was a great imperial port ruled by the British, the Americans, and the French with the aid of Chinese gangsters from the secret societies. In those days Shanghai had a well-earned reputation for sin, and the chief of its sins was cruelty. The foreigners who ruled Shanghai did not care what happened to the Chinese who worked for them. They provided no social programs, no free hospitals, no unemployment benefits. Their cruelty sprang from indifference, and they appeared to think that Shanghai and all the wealth of China would remain in their possession for everlasting. The Chinese who worked with the foreigners were no better. Huge stores of relief supplies lay on the wharves. They came from United Nations relief organizations and were plainly marked UNRRA. At night trucks drove up to these mountains of supplies and carted them away to the warehouses of Chinese generals. Only a trickle of relief supplies reached the Chinese people for whom they were intended.

It was as though there was a curse on Shanghai: everything about the city was evil. On one winter night three hundred Chinese men, women, and children were found frozen to death. There was poverty and malnutrition on a scale that exceeded anything one could imagine. The compradores and the old China Hands would tell you: "Think how much worse it would be if we were not here." And the truth was that it could not have been worse, that it was unimaginable that anything worse could happen to a city. I thought of it as a city that was dying, beyond salvation.

When the Chinese Communists entered Shanghai, they scarcely knew what to do with it. At one time they made plans to abandon it, to close it up, to forget that it existed. Its chief function was to serve as a port for international trade, and China in the early days of the Communist Revolution had almost no foreign trade. But even without foreign trade the city had a life of its own, urgent and demanding. It went on growing. Today the Chinese claim that it has a population of ten million and is the largest city in the world.

We reached the Hoping Hotel at about ten o'clock at night. We were a rather undistinguished-looking group moving through the lobby of the hotel, drab and down-at-heels and rather quiet, scarcely knowing or caring what lay in store for us, for we wanted to sleep away the aches and pains of the train journey from Hangchow. We had to wait a long time for our rooms. In the lobby there was a bookrack with free copies of Mao Tse-tung's little red book and the latest issues of the *Peking Review* in four or five languages. The atmosphere was subdued, somnolent. It appeared that everyone had gone to bed and the night porters had vanished.

We entered the hotel through an unpretentious door on a side street. The lobby too looked unpretentious. Some old women were sweeping the floors; a bellboy was reading a newspaper but there was not enough light and he kept shifting his position in order to see better. I thought it was a third- or fourth-rate hotel until I turned a corner and saw another lobby with marble columns and a high ceiling, and realized that I was back again in the Cathay Hotel, once the most prestigious hotel in Shanghai, where the Sassoons and the Kadoories attended board meetings and decided the affairs of the city. In those days, at ten o'clock in the evening, the lobby would be full of men in evening dress and elegantly gowned women, a hotel band would be playing, hotel servants would be rushing about, and the air would be electric with excitement. Rolls-Royces drew up at the main entrance facing the Bund. American generals with ten rows of medals sat drinking highballs in the palm court, and Chinese prostitutes with brilliantly painted faces walked languorously among the palms, usually with an old woman in tow who served as a selling agent. Boys, too, were for sale. I remembered painted frescoes on the walls, but they had gone. Gone, too, were the hotel servants who wore white gowns and mandarin caps of black silk, and bowed interminably. Gone, too, was the restaurant with the crystal chandeliers and the former Russian admiral who permitted you to enter only if you were wearing evening dress. Gone were the bright lights and the easy smiles and the gleam of diamonds seen from the other end of the lobby. I remembered arcades of mirrors, which made the lobby seem twenty times larger than it was, but they too had gone. Even the furniture had gone, for these heavily stuffed armchairs and sofas would not have been tolerated in the Cathay Hotel.

I confess I was not sorry they had gone, but it was strange to find the place so dark and empty. I went back to the smaller lobby and began to read the *Peking Review* in the hope of finding some news from the outside world. But the outside world was notably absent except for an article condemning the Soviet Union in general and another article condemning the Smith regime in Rhodesia in particular. One article caught my eye. It was headed "The People of Tachai and Hsiyang Denounce the Gang of Four," and it described a visit paid by Chiang Ching to a famous agricultural commune in Shansi shortly before Chairman Mao Tse-tung's death. According to the article she arrived in Tachai with a large retinue which included a truck loaded with cameramen and motion-picture equipment. Every night she watched "imported obscene films." When an urgent telegram arrived from the Central Committee, summoning her to Peking because her husband was in failing health and might die at any moment, she did not like a good wife hurry to his bedside; instead she played cards, joked, and delayed the journey as long as possible. The people of Tachai, according to the article, had other reasons to dislike her. She was in an ugly mood when she arrived. "I am here to fight," she said, and she accused the workers of Tachai of being complacent and politically backward and lacking respect for her. She ordered them to admit their faults; and when the leader of the revolutionary committee refused, she threw a tantrum. She had herself photographed beside a "wartime trench" dug by her aides on Tiger Hill, and when the photographic session was over, the villagers filled the trench and built a pigsty on the exact spot where she had been standing.

In the article the Gang of Four was accused of fomenting "all-out civil war" and of deliberately undermining the Great Proletarian Cultural Revolution. They were also accused of trying to restore capitalism and of deliberately casting suspicion on people they disliked in an effort to destroy them. "The vicious plot of the Gang of Four has been exposed and this gang of bloodsucking vermin, the scourge of the country and a calamity to the people, has been mercilessly condemned by history."

At last we received our room keys and were taken up to the fifteenth floor of the Hoping Hotel, which means "Peace Hotel." In the morning we looked down on the Bund and the Whangpoo River, which was steel-gray and resembled flowing metal. A hundred ships were sailing on the river, oil tankers, sampans, passenger ships, small coasting vessels, cargo boats, police launches darting about like maddened wasps. Seen from the gold-ceilinged dining room, the river seemed to be rushing downhill like a waterfall at sixty miles an hour.

On the Bund, too, there was ceaseless activity. People walk fast in Shanghai. There are not many buses, not many pedicabs, only a few taxis. So people learn to walk at a stinging pace. And looking down at the Bund, you have the illusion that there is no street, no sidewalk, no embankment: there is only a vast stream of people just as on the river there is a vast stream of ships.

We plunged down in the elevator to street level, to the

lobby which was once the most fashionable meeting place in Shanghai and was now nearly lifeless. You could buy postage stamps, handkerchiefs, whiskey, brandy, and souvenir postcards. There was a bookstall with the latest publications of the Foreign Languages Press. There were silk-embroidered portraits of Mao Tse-tung, Marx, and Lenin, imported from Hangchow. But the rather dark and cavernous lobby had only one essential purpose: to lead you into the street.

All along the Bund there were enormous posters denouncing Chiang Ching. The city was festooned with paper. The main entrance to the hotel had been boarded up, thus providing an admirable space for hanging up more posters. Armies of poster artists were being employed to write these "big-character" posters. In all the time I was in Shanghai I do not think there was any moment when it was not possible to see one of these posters. This was political propaganda on an immense and costly scale.

The huge gray buildings on the Bund, once the offices of bankers and merchant princes, were now the offices of party officials. These buildings that once celebrated the majesty of the colonial powers now looked shabby and obsolete, like dinosaurs washed up by the river. They had been deliberately designed to overpower; it was intended that they would last for a hundred years; they were well anchored in the marshy soil; they dominated by their sheer mass; and they looked like prisons. All that was worst in the Western world had come to Shanghai, including the architects. The more you examine these buildings the more you come to realize that in spite of their apparent strength, their deliberate brutality, the bronze lions guarding the gates, the huge and cavernous entrances, they are lacking in the grace that comes from real assurance. Mao Tse-tung was right when he described the foreign powers in China as "paper tigers."

And strangely the Russians have fallen into the same trap. During the honeymoon period between 1950 and 1960, when Russian engineers penetrated every quarter of China and when it seemed that Russia and China were joined together in everlasting friendship, it was proposed that in the heart of Shanghai the Russians would build a great Palace of Sino-Soviet Friendship. For reasons that are not at all obscure the Russians built a skyscraper taller than any of the buildings on the Bund. They were determined that their palace should excel all other palaces. So they built a gilded skyscraper with a slender gold spire a hundred feet high, and took elements from the Admiralty Spire and the vaults of St. Isaac's Cathedral in Leningrad, from the window embrasures of Byzantine churches, the columns of the Smolny Convent, and the gingerbread decor of a hundred other places, and built a towering birthday cake as pretentious and ugly as the new university in Moscow, and were a little surprised when the Chinese remarked that it seemed to be out of place in Shanghai. This building, too, lacks the grace that comes from real assurance. When the Russians left China, the great Palace of Sino-Soviet Friendship remained to testify to the brevity of friendship and the determination of the Russians to build cloud-capped palaces where they were not wanted. The huge palace dominates Shanghai and threatens to outlast the crumbling skyscrapers on the Bund.

"You have to understand," a friend said, "that the Chinese Communists were always a little disconcerted by the huge buildings left by their feudal forerunners. The mansions of the merchant princes were converted into children's palaces, and this was all the easier because there were usually large gardens for the children to play in. Thus Eli Kadoorie's property on the outskirts of Shanghai became a children's palace. But what do you do when you have a neat, compact palace without extensive gardens?

It is too big for them, it costs too much to maintain, it is just a nuisance. They struggle with the problem and sometimes they wonder whether it would not be better just to blow it up."

We visited Eli Kadoorie's palatial mansion which now belongs to the Shanghai municipality. Today about two thousand children are being taught there, learning everything from music and singing, to foreign languages, shipbuilding, and electrical engineering. It is a happy place. The children look freshly scrubbed, they chatter merrily, and are perfectly at ease in the broad corridors of the mansion. Most of them seem to be between the ages of nine and thirteen, but there were a few older boys in the engineering departments. The children wear brightly colored clothes, being the happy exceptions to the rule that everyone must wear drab Mao uniforms tightly buttoned at the neck. We watched them singing and dancing, performing acrobatics and engaging in traditional Chinese swordplay with wooden swords. They played music on Western instruments and on ancient Chinese instruments. They painted and drew caricatures, put on puppet shows, spoke English with singsong accents, and generally behaved with good manners and total concentration on their arts and crafts. They were not wasting their time attacking the Gang of Four, and there was little evidence of politics except for the obligatory portrait of Mao Tse-tung on the walls. They smiled easily and were self-assured. They were the happiest children we saw in China.

In former times the palace was known as the Marble House and belonged to the multi-millionaire Eli Kadoorie, who came to Shanghai in the nineties of the last century, made his first fortune in tramways, then branched out into real estate and into shipping and a hundred other profitable undertakings. He built a palace fit for a king and fit for children.

No. 3 Hospital

All Chinese hospitals give an impression of quietness and order, and of truly dedicated doctors and nurses, and it is in the nature of things that politics stops at their gates. Inevitably there will be a revolutionary committee and just as inevitably there will be one doctor who serves as the local party boss and is immediately recognizable because he speaks with an air of absolute authority, a stern and uncompromising man chosen by the party elite precisely because he is stern and uncompromising. But in a hospital—and only in a hospital—there is the feeling that the party no longer possesses absolute authority, that it is totally irrelevant, and that once it has penetrated the hospital walls it is nothing more than a self-perpetuating bureaucracy busily shifting papers from one side of the desk to the other and back again. It cannot function because it is concerned with government, and in a hospital only the doctors and the nurses can govern the patients.

Inevitably the party boss made his appearance. He sat stiffly in a well-padded Mao jacket at the head of a long table, a red-faced man, powerfully built, with a harsh raucous voice, reciting the litany we had heard many times before: that all the accomplishments of the hospital were due to the incessant study of Mao Tse-tung's teaching and consequently every single member of the medical staff was engaged in the battle of overcoming the Gang of Four; that the hospital was working under the guidance of Mao Tse-tung and the revolutionary committee; that every department of the hospital was impregnated with the spirit of communism and that we would be hopelessly misled if we believed otherwise. He was a pediatrician, and we were told by other doctors that he was a good man in his profession. They said nothing about his abilities as boss of the revolutionary committee, and I suspect that he was one of those bureaucrats who were especially detested by Mao Tse-tung.

Like many bureaucrats the doctor liked hearing himself speak, and so for a long time he expatiated on the particular virtues of No. 3 Hospital, the high quality of the medical service (80 percent of the operations were successful) and the high quality of the barefoot doctors who were trained here and sent out all over China. "Of course," he said, "we follow the teachings of our great leader Mao Tse-tung in employing both Chinese and Western medicine." He mentioned acupuncture, promised that we would soon be permitted to see a major operation on a patient who would remain awake throughout the operation, and went on talking.

Acupuncture fascinated us: most of us had read the books and pamphlets devoted to it, and we remained mystified. Acupuncture was often successful, but there was no plausible explanation. It had begun about 475 B.C. when some doctors discovered that when you puncture the fleshy area between the thumb and forefinger, pain in other parts of the body diminishes or vanishes altogether. At that time the only surgical instruments they possessed were sharp stones. Many years passed, and they began to use silver needles. By A.D. 220 the word had found a place in the dictionary. At some time between A.D. 265 and A.D. 429 there appeared the first manual of acupuncture, listing 649 specific points on the human body where needles can be inserted with benefit to the health. An intricate art had emerged, based on hundreds of thousands of experimental findings. When they first encountered it, Western doctors were horrified and thought of it as a peculiar kind of Chinese mumbo-jumbo. Only in the last twenty years have they begun to take it seriously.

I first encountered acupuncture in a small village on the

Chialing River thirty miles upstream from Chungking in 1942. It was market day. The storytellers, the sellers of lanterns, of gewgaws, quack medicines, and strange unguents were all sitting in the shade of a ginkgo tree on a little bluff overlooking the flooded river. From one of the branches of the ginkgo tree there hung a painted cloth chart of the human body drawn so sketchily that it was scarcely recognizable: it was more like a caricature of the human body. There were about two hundred points marked on it. A powerfully built middle-aged man in a dirty blue tattered gown was examining a young peasant woman who had disrobed to the waist and was standing there in the dappled sunlight. The acupuncturist removed a long silver needle from his pocket, accidentally dropped it, picked it up, wiped it on the gown, and then stuck it in the woman just above her left breast. Because he had dropped it and wiped it on his filthy gown, I assumed the woman would die of blood poisoning. I remember turning away in horror and hoping I would never see an acupuncturist again.

But here in No. 3 Hospital in Shanghai there was not the slightest doubt that acupuncture had been mastered, that it was an art and possessed formidable healing power. The doctors knew what they were doing; they even knew that acupuncture sometimes failed as inexplicably as it succeeded. Not very long ago they had made their first considerable advance in methodology. They had discovered that a needle twirling electrically was far more effective than a needle that was simply pushed into the flesh and left there. Further, the electric needle would be inserted at an angle. The calculation of angles and rate of twirl would be left to a new generation of acupuncturists.

We were given white caps and white surgical gowns and then led to a small glass-enclosed balcony overlooking the operating theater. The patient was a forty-year-old woman with an ovarian cyst. She lay on the table, her face in shadow immediately below us, the abdomen brilliantly lit by two powerful lamps, while the masked surgeons and nurses already hovered over her. We learned that the needles had already been inserted in her back and were twirling satisfactorily: she was already under acupuncture anesthesia. Yet she was wide awake, her eyes open, and she gazed up at us without any emotion. She had a rather heavy round face of great dignity and composure. A doctor was saying: "In about 10 percent of the patients we find that acupuncture simply doesn't work for major operations. In that case we give them regular anesthetics. We shall know very soon if this patient is susceptible to acupuncture anesthesia."

The light over her abdomen was so bright that it was almost blinding. A knife flashed, ripping the belly open in one slash. A little blood spilled in a thin line and was mopped away. The woman smiled bravely and looked drowsy: there was no indication that she had felt any pain, no clenching of the facial muscles, no tightening of the jaw.

For a while, in the contemplation of the drama taking place under the intense bright lights, we forgot the woman. There were two doctors and two nurses, gowned and hooded, but we were scarcely aware of their presence. We saw a pair of rubber-gloved hands dancing over the wound, widening it, probing it, and sometimes one of the hands would vanish entirely within the wound, as though there was a vast, capacious emptiness within her, and we were aware of fingers moving under the surface. Then for about five minutes these disembodied hands performed the long and complicated dance of tying up the sutures, and more hands appeared, like dancers rushing in from the wings. Every movement of the dance was carefully choreographed.

A doctor on the balcony was saying: "She has been told

to breathe deeply. She is in no pain. Everything will be all right."

The abdomen became bloodier, the blood pumping up like a fountain. Quite suddenly everything seemed to be getting worse, as though deep inside something totally unexpected was happening. The hands danced more quickly: at one time there were four hands hovering over the wound or plunged into it. We looked at the woman's face in the shadows: she was still smiling her drowsy smile. The wound, originally a thin straight line, was now four or five inches wide, and resembled a bloody soup full of chunks of meat, and all of them were in movement. The surgeon dealt with them firmly: the chunks that were struggling to get out were pushed back firmly. All the time he was burrowing deeper, searching for the cyst and its roots. And suddenly the cyst emerged, as though it had swum up from the depths, covered with blood, grotesque and shapeless like an enormous blood clot, but within an instant the blood drained away and we saw the cyst as it really was—an enormous white silvery pearl nearly six inches in diameter, beautiful, with mysterious lights in it, layer upon layer of light glowing in its depths. For nearly a minute it remained there, cradled in the surgeon's hand, while with the other hand he searched for the root, examining the bloody cavity from which it emerged.

What was surprising was the sheer beauty of the cyst as he held it up to the light. It was like the elevation of the host, so bright and pure a thing that it seemed to have nothing to do with the world of pain and suffering. When the root was cut at last, he lifted it higher in the air so that we could see it better, and as he brought it closer to the light it glowed more splendidly.

"She will need rest," the doctor was saying. "In a week she will be walking about. Of course we have to take abdominal surgery very seriously, especially since abdominal operations under acupuncture anesthesia are less successful than operations on the brain and heart. This is another problem we have not solved. Why should one be more successful than the other? We don't know, but we are trying to find out."

The drama was coming to an end. For a few more moments we saw the enormous pearl shining in the doctor's hand and then it was laid in a dish and carried out of sight.

In ancient days the Chinese believed that people who were pure and innocent secreted pearls inside themselves. It was a mark of divine favor. Virgins who died young and great saints were distinguished by having these pearls, which were discovered when their bodies were cremated. Whenever I heard this story, I would ask what happened to the pearls found in the ashes. Since no one seemed to know, I assumed that it happened very rarely, so rarely indeed that no one ever saw them.

The Bronzes

At some time during the fifteenth century B.C. the Chinese began to make sacrificial vessels of bronze in the small area dominated by the Shang emperors. They are vessels of great beauty and power with representations of a sacred animal, who may be the Siberian tiger, in abstract form. We see the bulging eyes, the curling claws, the teeth, the pointed ears, but they are not arranged in a naturalistic form. The artists have rearranged the forms to suggest the utmost power, producing an object that is almost pure force. These sacrificial vessels were made in about twenty shapes, from tall and slender wine goblets to vast bellying containers of meat and grain, and although these shapes changed a little over the centuries the essential elements remained unchanged. Even in the Ching dynasty, thirty-five centuries later, the same objects continued to be made, though not in bronze but in jade.

These bronzes, often bearing archaic inscriptions, have been found in ancient tombs, and they are treasured by museums and collectors, who are prepared to pay phenomenal prices for them because they are becoming increasingly rare. The Chinese Communist government will not allow them to be exported; they are regarded rightly as belonging to the Chinese people; they are among the earliest treasures, all the more prized because they demonstrate the artistic skill of the Chinese bronzesmiths at the beginning of history.

There is a museum in Shanghai which has one of the world's most impressive collections of Chinese bronzes. It stands on a crowded, busy street, and there is not the slightest indication from outside that you are about to enter a museum. There is a narrow lobby; an elevator that can hold two people comfortably takes you to the second floor, and you step out into a room filled with a glittering display of ancient bronze weapons. Beyond this, in room after room, stand the great bronze wine vessels and ceremonial vessels of all kinds used by the Shang emperors and their tributary kings during the ritual sacrifices. There are about four hundred of these vessels, and the mind reels at their splendor.

Ancient Chinese bronzes are an acquired taste, and there is a good deal to be said for acquiring it. We still tend to think of Chinese art as the epitome of delicacy and refinement. These bronzes are so powerful that they resemble bombs about to explode. There is a barbaric delicacy in them, a sense of urgency and rock-ribbed strength, a fierce grace. We know that they were placed on bronze altars, usually in groups of three, and that offerings to the gods were made from them, while the priests chanted. Some of them have inscriptions inside: the shorter the inscription the older they are. Some resemble urns, others are like cooking pots, and still others are shaped like animals. A fluted object called a *k'u* would serve as a flower vase; it is in fact a goblet. The twenty established shapes which were copied through the centuries become progressively weaker, losing bit by bit their grace and authority. They also made bronze musical bells ranging from three feet high to a few inches, and these bells have curious projections like bullets to increase their resonance. When they were made, these vessels shone like gold and were highly polished. Now with their green patina they are more beautiful than they were in the time of the Shang emperors.

You rarely see these vessels outside museums, for the good reason that they are almost beyond price. Recently a small *fang-i*, a grain container shaped like a box with a capped roof, sold in New York for $480,400. On the antique market the objects in the Shanghai museum would scarcely sell for less than $100 million. They will not be sold, for the Chinese Communist government has clamped down on the export of antiques, except those that are hardly worth buying.

So we walked with our mouths agape beside the glass cases where the treasures of the Shang dynasty were on display. None of us knew the precise significance of these vessels, but it was not difficult to realize their sacramental power and the richness of invention which went into their making. Chinese civilization started out from strength. There was no early fumbling stage in the making of bronzes, or at least no one has yet discovered it. Here is power in a compact space shaped by artists in a civilization that was rounded and complete. It would be dangerous to underestimate the power of the Chinese who produced these objects.

Sated with these splendors, we asked the museum director where we would find the paintings, sculptures, and ceramics which we knew were in the museum.

"You have seen enough," he said sternly. "The rest of the museum is closed for repair."

For once there was no argument. We crowded into the tiny elevator and walked out into the roaring street.

The Friendship Shop

The British consulate general in Shanghai was one of those imposing edifices built at a time when the British were at the height of their imperial power. Like the Hong Kong and Shanghai Bank, which was not far away along the Bund, it was built to last for centuries. It was not an especially ornate building, no huge lions stood at the entrance, it did not need to breathe authority: it *was* authority. It was imposing chiefly because it was very large and because it was surrounded by an enormous well-kept garden.

I remembered this building with mixed feelings, for in 1946 I attempted to get some help from the consulate general to obtain a visa. It was obvious that they regarded visas with polite indifference; they had more serious matters to attend to. I was annoyed, demanded to see the consul general, saw him, got the matter straightened out, and was leaving when he called after me: "I hear you have been in Yenan. What is it like up there?" I said: "They will be here very soon." He clapped his knee. "That's the best joke I have heard in a month of Sundays!" he exclaimed.

"The Chinese Communists here! What in God's name do you think they will be able to do with this place?"

He was not the only Englishman who thought the Chinese Communists would shrivel up in their caves.

Well, the Chinese Communists were here, but the British consulate general appeared to have vanished. I walked along the Bund in search of it. I thought I knew exactly where to find it. It was not where I thought it was, and I gave up searching for it. One day I visited the Friendship shop, a kind of PX reserved for foreigners, set back in a large garden along the Bund. It was a four-story building of no great antiquity, perhaps four or five years old, resembling a department store. On the three occasions I visited the Friendship Shop there were only a few foreigners moving about in its vast emptiness. On the second occasion I asked about the British consulate general. It was obviously somewhere near, but exactly where? The answer was: "You are standing on it, or rather you are not standing on it."

This was confusing, but the two statements could be reconciled without too much difficulty. The consulate general had been sacked and set on fire in 1966, at the time of the Great Proletarian Cultural Revolution. The Red Guards went about its destruction with determination and nothing was left except cinders. The Shanghai municipal council sought to find a worthy use for the site and considered transforming it into a public garden. Instead it was decided to erect the Friendship Shop in the corner of the garden, and since only foreigners were permitted to enter the shop the ghost of extraterritoriality still hovered over it.

The top story of the Friendship Shop was reserved for antiques, all bearing the little red seal without which they were not permitted to leave the country. There were not many genuine antiques, there was nothing more than a hundred years old, and nothing very valuable. But at least there were scroll paintings, all neatly rolled up, and one could spend a leisurely hour unrolling them, hoping to find a good painting. Most of them were bad, but occasionally there was one a little out of the ordinary. The prices were clearly marked, there was no bargaining, they were being sold like slabs of cheese. Finally, after unrolling nearly a hundred paintings, I found a presentable copy of a painting by the Yuan dynasty master Ni Tsan—a straw-roofed hut and some ragged trees in the foreground with misty mountains looming far in the distance. Ni Tsan spent his life wandering in a boat along all the rivers of eastern China in an effort to escape from the tyranny of the Mongol invaders, and his paintings reflect the silence of the rivers and the lonely trees growing on the edge of sandbanks. In Ni Tsan's world it is nearly always autumn, the trees have shed their leaves, they are stiffening a little against the coming storms. No people walk through his paintings: only the empty landscape, and the barren trees stark against the skyline. These trees are man's surrogates, they stand watch, they endure.

With the painting under my arm I walked out of the compound of the former British consulate general into the raging traffic of Shanghai, the crowds milling on the narrow sidewalks, the hundreds of bicyclists, the trucks charging through them, the loudspeakers blaring denunciations of Chiang Ching, the wall posters that were wrapping up the whole city as though it were a parcel, and the screaming steam whistles of the ships on the Whangpoo River. Ni Tsan's painting was the sheer antithesis of everything that Shanghai represented. It is silence, contemplation, humility, withdrawal from the world, and it was good to find such a painting in the heart of the roaring city.

Conversation with Lao Wu

I shall call him Lao Wu, which is not his real name, though it is a name he would recognize. He came from an old Mandarin family in Tientsin and was once wealthy, living in a large house with many servants and retainers. I remember that he employed a superb cook, who was almost as famous as his art collection, which was especially rich in ancient bronzes and Sung paintings. He had a long, rather heavy face which was once ivory-white and was now like parchment thinly drawn over the bones, for he was in his seventies. He had powerful shoulders and he used to say that he resembled a coolie who could pull a load of cement over all the mountains of China. Even now, dressed in a frayed blue Mao jacket, he looked like an aristocrat.

We met in a restaurant on Nanking Road and talked for four hours. I asked him how he lived and he said: "In one room. You don't believe it? It's true. One small room up four flights of stairs. A chair, a bed, a shelf of books, two paintings, nothing else. I have a small pension. The government looks after me. I don't think about the past. I am absolutely content. Of course I still paint a little, but much less than in former times. I cook my own meals. I would like you to see my room, but the street committee would probably not approve of it, or I would have to get special permission, there would be meetings and discussions, and finally they might say: 'No, he cannot see your room. What reason has he to see your room?' They wouldn't understand. In the old days our rooms were part of ourselves, but now our rooms are assigned to us by committees. The street committee rules us. We do what they say, and since they represent the combined wisdom of the street, what they say is usually quite sensible."

I tried to imagine Lao Wu's single room up four flights of steps in a working-class quarter of Shanghai. Was there a window? Was there a view? What color were the walls? Was there a table? How could he paint without a table? Carpets, rugs? Where was the lavatory? He smiled broadly: "I understand. You want to see me in my room. Very easy. I will do a sketch and send it to you. It's very small—about six feet by eight feet."

It was on the tip of my tongue to say there are prison cells larger than that, but I said nothing.

"You forget that our population is expanding. There are ten million people in Shanghai. We have to crowd up a bit. I have absolutely no regrets about that. Of course, I would prefer to live in Peking, but Peking is changed so much that I would be uncomfortable there. They have torn down the walls—I don't know why. They were so beautiful and they gave us a feeling of protection. Tell me, what did they gain by tearing down the walls?"

It occurred to me that when I was last in Peking the walls were still standing, and I could remember walking along them with a sense of perfect freedom, looking down at the teeming Chinese city, and beyond the city lay the ripening fields and the distant mountains.

"Have they all gone?" I asked.

"Yes. It is called urban renovation or something like that, and they had five or six committees to study the problem. Well, the committees came to different conclusions. Some concluded that some of the walls should be torn down and that others should remain, while others concluded that the walls should remain and indeed that they should be reinforced. And then—and this is the story that was told to me—the problem was taken to Chairman Mao Tse-tung. As you know, he was the great simplifier. He said: 'Let them all come down!' Just like that! They even began to destroy the gate towers. He saw them working on one of the gate towers and asked them what they were doing. He was told they were tearing it down, and he flew into a temper and said: 'Next you will be tearing down the Forbidden City.' They thought this was an order and said that when they were finished with the gate tower they would turn their attention to the Forbidden City, if he gave the order. He was so enraged that he actually hit one of the workmen, and said: 'Do you understand, nothing must be torn down! Now it is time to build!'"

There was a pause, and then he said: "What frightens me is that if Chairman Mao Tse-tung had given the order to tear down the Forbidden City, it would have been done. Excellent reasons would have been found for it—the feudal past must be torn up by the roots, and so on. There would have been big-character writings: 'We are ashamed to live in the presence of the thieving emperors.' They would have destroyed the Forbidden City. It would have been very easy and all over in a week! And then where would we be? The Forbidden City is our glory! It is useless to destroy the past because it will always catch up with us. I believe that in time we shall study our past—not the remote past of the archeologists, but the last thousand years when, even though we had an emperor, we experimented and pondered and wrote memorials to the emperor and decisions were not made by a single fallible being but by a consensus of scholars."

"Do you think the scholars will come back?"

"Yes, but they will not be the scholars who pass the imperial examinations. It will be another kind of examination altogether, just as rigorous but directed to another end. They would learn sociology, not poetry."

He said a little later: "We are still evolving. Chinese communism is not standing still. Outwardly it appears to be static, formed, finished. It was crystallized around the person of Chairman Mao Tse-tung. It was as though the whole country had become a reflection of his ideas, his imagination, his will. And we needed it, or at least we needed it in the early stages. But, you understand, now that he is dead, we cannot live eternally under his shadow. There will be new ideas and freedom to utter them. The party leaders will pay lip service to him, they will quote from his works or discover new unpublished quotations, but even now it is becoming difficult to quote from his works, for he said many contradictory things. What will remain will not be his works so much as the man himself with all his contradictions."

At some point in the discussion I said I was puzzled by the phrase *following the capitalist road,* which was applied to Chiang Ching. I could not understand how anyone could be a capitalist in China any more than it was possible to be a landowner, for the state owns all the capital and all the land.

"You ask this in Shanghai?" he smiled.

"Is there something special in Shanghai?"

"Of course there is! Capitalism dies hard! Remember, this is not an egalitarian state, and Chairman Mao Tse-tung never proclaimed that it was his duty to bring about an egalitarian state. It may be—it probably is—more egalitarian than any existing state, but there are people in Shanghai who are still amassing fortunes. There are men who make nine hundred yuan a month, they can save money and lend it out at interest. It is against the law but they do it. In China nine hundred yuan a month is the beginning of a fortune!"

Now 900 yuan equals about $530, and there are people on welfare in New York who receive as much.

"You must remember we live on a different scale," he

went on. "Here a bowl of rice costs almost nothing, rent costs nothing, bus fares cost almost less than nothing, clothes are expensive, but how many suits of clothes can you buy in a year? Entertainment is cheap. For one yuan you can have a good seat in the theater, though I am not sure there is anything worth seeing. Money? I think it will vanish altogether in China within twenty years. There will be no need for it."

We talked about his paintings and calligraphy, for he had been a famous painter and his calligraphy was prized and once sold for enormous sums.

"I am no longer allowed to sell my paintings," he said. "Up to the time of the Great Proletarian Cultural Revolution, there were provisions for artists to sell their paintings. Now I give them away to my friends. If they like the paintings, they may give me a present—eggs, a piece of cloth, a piece of brocade. The truth is that the government has failed miserably to address itself to the problem of the arts. Artists, of course, are still recruited. Someone has to do the terrible propaganda drawings you see in the streets. Artists are employed in embroidery factories to make designs, and in porcelain factories and things like that. They do what they are told to do. It is the same with writers— they cannot have their works published unless they are approved by government committees. The imagination has been imprisoned. Nevertheless some painters continue painting, and there are some poets who continue to write poems that circulate in manuscript."

"Like *samizdat* in Russia?"

"No, on a very much smaller scale. There is no organized opposition in China, none that I know of. The workers are unhappy because there has been no raise of wages in fifteen years. Many, many things have gone wrong, but no one protests, or rather they protest very fitfully. When things get really bad, they explode. The army is called in, the explosion dies down, and everything goes on as before."

I asked him whether he was free to travel anywhere in China.

"Yes, of course."

"You could take the Peking train this evening, if you wanted to?"

"Yes, why not?"

"No restrictions whatsoever?"

"Of course I would consult the street committee. I would have to make arrangements for someone to water my plants and look after my cat. Things like that. We don't have internal passports. The street committee has enormous power if it wants to use it, but it very rarely uses it. If I had a very good reason for going to Peking, they would say 'Go' and think nothing of it."

"But you would consult them?"

"Of course, but only because of my plants and my cat."

"What happened to your art collection?"

"The government took it."

"Were you sorry?"

"No. What on earth can a man do with an art collection? I had enjoyed it for nearly half a century. I felt it was time for the people to enjoy it. They let me catalog it and then they took it away in boxes. I have absolutely no regrets about this."

"Where can we see the paintings?"

"I can't tell you. The government has them—they are still in boxes, I imagine. One day they will take them out. I believe they are absolutely safe. For me, this is the important thing. In God's good time the people will be able to see them. In any case I never had the feeling that my art collection belonged to me."

We were sitting in a small booth on the second floor of

the restaurant which was all plain boards, solid tables and bamboo chairs, with no ornament anywhere. A small crowd gathered near the booth, to watch us. It was a friendly crowd, very quiet, gazing with a kind of detached interest at a foreigner and a mandarin. I was scarcely aware of them until it occurred to me that they were breathing all the oxygen in the neighborhood and I was close to fainting. Lao Wu waved them away, but they came back again.

"It's probably against the law for you to eat in this restaurant," Lao Wu said. "These people haven't been near to a foreigner for years. Don't worry—you are providing them with entertainment."

"How?"

"Just by being here."

I asked him what happened to his immense house in Tientsin.

"It burned down," he said very calmly, as though the burning of a house was a daily occurrence. "This happened shortly after I gave the art collection to the government. If I had seen the art collection going up in flames I would have gone mad! It happened two or three days later. The Tientsin fire brigade is inefficient, the house burned down to the ground, and I was left with absolutely nothing. I think this was absolutely the best thing that could have happened!"

"No regrets?"

"None at all. The house was a place to hang my paintings in, and when the paintings were gone the house had lost its meaning."

We had come to the restaurant for a late lunch, and it was now early evening. The lights were coming up, and the waiters were getting ready for the crowds who would soon be trooping in. We walked down the wooden stairway into the dark street. A bus passed. Lao Wu shouted over his shoulder: "Let's catch it!" and we raced for the bus stop. With those powerful shoulders that could pull a load of cement over the mountains of China, he shouldered his way into the crowded bus. "You understand, I am a proletarian now," he said.

Pumpkin Lane

In 1937 the Japanese army and navy decided to crush China and establish a continental empire. In the following years they established their empire, occupying more than half of China, looting and burning everything in their path until they felt safe enough to install a puppet regime in Nanking. It was a war unlike any war up to that time: the chief instrument was massacre. They killed indiscriminately, tirelessly, unthinkingly. It was as though mass killing had become a habit, and there was no end to it.

Some of the most terrible massacres took place in Shanghai beyond the International Settlements. The Japanese had thirty-two ships anchored in the river, and an army of two hundred thousand men on shore. In three months of battles large areas of suburban Shanghai became uninhabitable deserts. One day observers in Shanghai looked in the direction of the working-class suburb of Chapei. It had vanished. Instead there was a six-mile wall of flame.

Such things happened often during the Sino-Japanese War, which is now largely forgotten. Even the Chinese are beginning to forget the many wars they fought against the Japanese, but a few survivors from the Chapei massacre have not forgotten. They are still living in Chapei. They sometimes come to look at a large blown-up aerial photograph which shows Chapei as it was after the flames had burned themselves out—black and wrinkled like an immense tar pit. The photograph is in a small office in Pumpkin Lane, a housing project built by the Shanghai municipality in 1963.

It was a good place to go because the people who lived there appeared to be enjoying a life of their own. It was a community with its own way of life, its own institutions, its own hopes. Among these hopes was that the community would not grow bigger, and would not be swallowed up by neighboring communities. There were 35 blocks of five-story houses, 1,018 households, and a population of 8,000. "This is manageable," said the earnest middle-aged woman who headed the revolutionary committee. "If it gets larger, it will not be manageable. We want to keep it the way it is." It was as though they had found the ideal proportions of a small city—a thousand households.

Pumpkin Lane was provided with all the necessities of life—a nursery, a kindergarten, a primary school, food shops, a barbershop, a bank, a workshop, and a cooperative medical center. The people looked well fed; the children were dressed in bright colors; no one was hurrying. There was even a suggestion that Pumpkin Lane was a kind of backwater, remote from the turmoil of Shanghai, where everyone seemed to be making up for lost time. There was also a suggestion that the housing project had taken its tone from the head of the revolutionary committee. She was a small woman with very high cheekbones and little slit-eyes, but she was demonstrably human, warm, determined, and intelligent, and in this she differed from most of the heads of revolutionary committees we had seen. She did not look like a bureaucrat. She did not dominate. She spoke quietly of her thousand families as though she knew all of them. Behind her was the blown-up photograph of the black tar pit.

The Japanese destroyed Chapei, and Chapei went on living. Squatters came and built a village out of mud, jute bags, and mat-sheds. Mostly they were refugees from Kansu and Anhui who were accustomed to hunger. Somehow they survived the Japanese occupation which came to an end in 1945 and Chiang Kai-shek's government which came to an end in 1949. The Chinese Communists had pressing problems to deal with, and three years passed before they got around to Chapei. The four-foot-high mud huts were torn down, and they began to build somewhat larger huts with tie roofs and wooden walls for a people so accustomed to poverty that the sight of new wood drove them almost frantic. They had lived by begging, picking through garbage, pulling rickshaws. One of the architects of the new shanty town decided that two or three of the old huts should be preserved—a monument to poverty, a reminder of an inglorious past. These huts, made of burlap, jute bags and mud, survive in a small corner of Pumpkin Lane. "We lived in those huts for ten years," a woman said. "Just here, twenty feet away, I gave birth to a baby in the open air."

In 1963 the Chinese Communist government began to think seriously about Chapei. There were urgent reasons for doing so. The small wooden huts were no great improvement on the huts made of mud. Chapei was still festering. Within six months all the huts were torn down and the five-story buildings went up. On July 16, 1964, came the official opening: processions, flags, the beating of drums and cymbals. Then at last Chapei rose from the ashes.

We wandered around Pumpkin Lane, visited some of the householders, climbed the concrete steps, went in and out of living rooms and bedrooms, and saw so many children that we sometimes wondered whether the limit of two children per family was not being exceeded. "Women hold up half the sky," Mao Tse-tung had said, and we had the impression that women had a good deal to say about the running of the community. The place was calm and orderly. One of the householders said: "We are lucky. We have very many old people among us and they take care of the children." It seemed that in every apartment there were old grandparents and very young children.

It was here in Chapei that we saw the oldest man we saw in China. They said he was ninety-three. He was a fine figure of a man with powerful features and a small white beard, very upright. But the most extraordinary thing about him was his costume, for he wore a long stiff gown of some gray material and a black *makua*, a kind of vest, belonging to an age that has long since departed. He also wore a black silken skullcap which, if it had been decorated with a jewel, would have signified that he was a mandarin. He was standing at the corner of a road, waving his stick at some children who were calling to him, and there was something comic and endearing about his pretended rage. I asked where he had come from. No one seemed to know, although they knew his age and his name. For all his early life he had lived under the Manchus; he had seen the emperors come and go, and lived through a succession of revolutions, each more bloody than the one before it. He had survived it all and was strong enough to shake a stick at boys and girls who could have been his great-great-grandchildren. "Half-blind!" they said, but he did not look like a half-blind man as he walked down the dusty road in the new housing project in Chapei.

For me he was China incarnate, strong-shouldered, proud as the devil, as old as the hills, and carrying his great age lightly.

Professor Yang Chi-sheng

He was the first Chinese professor I came to know well, for he was the head of the English department at Fuhtan University when I went to teach there in 1942. At that time the university consisted of some cattle sheds erected on a bluff overlooking the swift-flowing Chialing River, thirty miles upstream from Chungking. Originally Fuhtan University had been in Shanghai; the professors and students marched across China to escape from the advancing Japanese.

Although there was a teaching staff there were almost no books and precious little equipment. But the students were eager to learn and full of enthusiasm for the new China that would come to birth when the Japanese had been swept out of their land. They were idealists to a degree I had not thought possible among a people who were generally pragmatic and down-to-earth. Professor Yang Chi-sheng was one of those who sometimes attempted to temper their idealism. He would say: "Keep your head on your shoulders. It is not going to be Paradise." Unrepentantly the students believed that Paradise would come about as soon as the Japanese went away.

The old professor came into my hotel room in Shanghai as though thirty years were only a few days. I had last seen him wearing a scholar's blue gown; now he wore a Mao jacket and trousers. His face was unlined; he had the same dazzling smile and he still gestured with his long hands and he still spoke English with a precise accentuation that was more common before World War I than after it. He used words like "beholden" and "betimes." I think his favorite English writers were Shakespeare, Jane Austen, and Trollope. He liked the early Hemingway, the Nick Adams stories, and wondered what went wrong in the later years. "I have read Mr. Saul Bellow's works," he said, "and I must say they read very well. Is he trying to say something?" Modern American literature puzzled him. Why so much violence? why the sense of doom? what had gone amiss? It was characteristic of him to use a word like "amiss." "We are out of touch," he went on. "I do not speak with any authority on American literature. There was a terrible violence in Melville and Hawthorne—in Emerson, too. So it was something bred very early into American literature. And the violence of the Vietnam War was unbelievable. I do not understand why people resort to violence."

I said there was violence in China, too. It was on the billboards and walls of every street in Shanghai in the ferocious denunciations of Chiang Ching. Such things could perhaps be explained, but they were acts of violence. He said cryptically: "If you had lived in Shanghai, you would understand why we have such a detestation of her," and refused to be drawn into further discussion of her. He said of Mao Tse-tung: "He laid down the principles by which men can live in dignity."

He was now long past the age of retirement, suffering from various ailments, slow in movement, frail but full of fire. He remembered that under Chiang Kai-shek the old were left to rot, made dependent on their families, but under the Communist regime the old were granted a special place in society. He still taught at Fuhtan University but he was more a counselor than a teacher. He was given a salary more than sufficient for his needs. He could afford small luxuries. "I want for nothing," he said, "but of course I don't live in this sort of luxury." He waved his arms at the hotel room with its overstuffed furniture and thread-bare carpet and two enormous beds, the long mirrors, the cavernous bathroom, the five-foot-high chest of drawers, and in the midst of all this ancient furniture there was a small delicately built glass-top table which had some pretensions to good design. "Horrible!" he said, dismissing the whole room with a wave of his hand. "I wonder that you can bring yourself to stay here?"

I said I would much prefer to be staying at Fuhtan University. When we were living near Chungking, we used to dream of the campus which was so vast, so beautiful, provided with so many shade trees and well-appointed laboratories, and with so many books in its libraries. The students spoke of going back to Shanghai as the Jews speak of going to Jerusalem. I had applied for permission to visit the university, and was told that it was quite impossible. Why? It would cause too much inconvenience. How? Because the entire faculty and student body was engaged in day-long criticisms of Chiang Ching. Wasn't this a waste of everybody's time? No. What would people say in America if the entire faculty and student body at Yale got together to criticize the president's widow not just for one day but for a week, for two weeks? I was reminded that Chinese universities are not like universities in America. In China a university is a political arm of the government and it does what the government orders it to do.

There were ghosts around us of long-dead students and long-dead professors. What had happened to the enormously fat professor who taught English in a high squeaky voice? Dead a long time ago. And the president of the university, who was stiff-necked and also straight-backed, and fought off the elaborate demands of the Kuomintang government? Dead long ago. And Professor Liang Tsongtai who came from a rich landlord family in Canton and was a friend of the French poet Paul Valéry? A superb athlete, he enjoyed climbing the Szechuan mountains at a pace that made us dizzy, and if we accompanied him, it was not for long. Soon enough he would be standing on a peak like a mountain goat, waving to us as we crawled along the valleys below. Dead? No. He was alive and vigorous in his late seventies, and still teaching in Canton at the Foreign Languages Institute. And Professor Chang Chi-yang, once dean of the law department in Fuhtan and formerly chief justice of the Shanghai Supreme Court, a crusty man with formidable charm, who adored the law—"Law is absolute"—and hated doctors—"They are all quacks!"—and when his hand became bright blue and swollen with blood poisoning announced that there were sufficient antibodies in the body to cure it and was not in the least surprised when the swelling went down and the hand became white again. What happened to him? He was in his nineties, living in retirement in Peking, as crusty as ever.

The thirty years vanished, and we were once more in the cattle sheds perched on the banks of the swift-flowing Chialing River in a valley between two gorges. Here in the valley the Indian corn grew eight feet high and there were little stone temples to the rice goddess among the rice fields. Nearby was a village with a single street called Huangchiushu (Yellow Tree Village), where I lived in a house with paper-thin walls for a month of misery. The village and everyone in it was owned by a fat landlord who was a caricature of power and wealth when he strolled down the street while the people bowed before him, terrified of him and the armed cutthroats who were his bodyguards. When a girl was found murdered, we assumed she had been murdered because she resisted his advances. It was in this street that I saw a dozen farm boys roped together and being led off to fight in Chiang Kai-shek's war, and the boys had bloody faces and all of them were weeping.

I asked Professor Yang whether he could remember the landlord's name. He shook his head. He said: "It is so long since we had any landlords in our country."

A few minutes later I saw him off in a taxi. It was late at night; the streets were nearly deserted; the strange smell of burned sugar hung in the air. The professor put on his small white face-mask, because, he explained, "there are so many noxious poisons in the atmosphere," and vanished into darkness. In another thirty years, when I come to Shanghai, he will still be there.

Present at the Creation

One day we were taken to the small building, once a girls' school in the French Concession of Shanghai, where the Chinese Communist party was founded on July 1, 1921. The small schoolhouse at 106 Hsin-yi Lu has become a shrine. An enormous red flag flies over it, and the crest of the Chinese Communist party has been carved in red sandstone over the four doors that lead out onto a narrow street.

Historians have had a good deal of trouble with the events that took place at the founding of the party. The documents were lost, or perhaps there were no documents. Tung Pi-wu, one of the founding members, wrote in his memoirs that Chen Tu-hsiu had been proposed as the chairman of the conference, but he happened to be in Canton and so a certain Chang Kuo-tao took his place. Chen Tu-hsiu was the founding father of Chinese communism, but was later deposed. Tung Pi-wu remembered that they drew up an anti-imperialist and anti-militarist manifesto, and discussed at some length whether government officials and technicians (skilled members of the bourgeoisie, factory managers, and engineers) should be permitted to join the party, and they apparently decided to exclude officials but to include technicians. It was agreed that the party should remain "pure and secret," and that the main task of party members was to recruit as many followers as possible. The aim of the party was to overthrow the existing government and to establish the dictatorship of the proletariat. Tung Pi-wu also remembered that two foreign Communists were present. One was Grigory Voitinsky, the head of the eastern department of the Communist International, who received his instructions directly from Lenin, and the other was Hendricus Sneevliet, known as Maring, a Dutch Communist who had recently been attempting to form a Communist party in the Dutch East Indies. Sneevliet later accompanied the Chinese Communists during part of the Long March, but he appears to have been very opinionated and somewhat contemptuous of his companions, and they were glad to be rid of him. He returned to Holland and was killed by the Germans when they invaded his country.

There were twelve Chinese Communists, one Russian, and one Dutchman at the founding of the party.* The girls' school was chosen because it was summer and the girls were away, while the fact that the school was in the French Concession meant that they were probably free from observation by the Chinese police. They met in a long class-

---

* The official list of the Chinese delegates shown to visitors at the shrine is as follows: (1) Mao Tse-tung, d. 1976, (2) Tung Pi-wu, d. 1975, (3) Wang Ching-mei, d.E. 1925, (4) Teng En-ming, d.E. 1931, (5) Chen Tu-hsiu, d. 1943, (6) Ho Shu-heng, d.E. 1935, (7) Li Han-chün, d.E. 1927, (8) Chang Kuo-tao, K, (9) Liu Jen-ching, (10) Chen Kung-po, K, (11) Chou Fu-hai, K, (12) Li Ta, d. 1966. d.E. means they were executed by the Kuomintang, and K means they went over to the Kuomintang. The list is probably inaccurate and at least three other delegates are known to have attended.

room, and the delegates sat in front of small desks facing a podium. On the third or fourth day—no one could remember exactly how long they remained at the girls' school, and even the exact date when they met is unknown—someone blundered into the school and said he was looking for a friend. There was something sinister about the appearance of the stranger; he was believed to be a police spy. The delegates therefore agreed to meet on a lake near Chiahsing and quickly abandoned the girls' school. They met a few days later on a rather luxurious houseboat on the lake and finished up their business before dispersing. The houseboat has been discovered and this too has become a shrine.

We spent about an hour in the room where the party was founded, listening to the head of the revolutionary committee in charge of it. He intoned the list of the delegates as a priest might intone the names of saints. He pointed out that we had come to the shrine of shrines and no other place in China was quite so sacred, while the sunlight poured through the window on the overstuffed chairs and the long table so highly polished that we could see our faces in it. For most of us, I think, the shrine suffered from a phenomenon common to many shrines in other parts of the world. Although obviously authentic, it was unconvincing. It no longer looked like a place where revolutionaries met in secret; it looked like the board room of high-powered executives.

"In those days," the head of the revolutionary committee was saying, "there were only seventy members of the Communist party in all of China. Now there are thirty million members."

NOTES FROM A DIARY

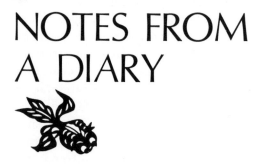

The great and good Johnny Fairchild was saying this morning that his mind is becoming numbed and he can no longer absorb what he sees and hears. I think this is true of all of us. Partly it is because we have heavy colds but it is also because we are on the move all day, going from schools and factories to communes and museums, without any time to think and brood, to take stock, to think out the problems to a conclusion. There is also the heavy hammering of propaganda constantly repeated in exactly the same words deadening in their intensity. When we sit at the long white tables and listen over cups of tea to the schoolteachers or the factory directors as they describe their achievements made possible only by the genius of "our great teacher and leader Mao Tse-tung," we are exhausted almost before they have begun. We know what they are going to say, and it is always the same.

What disturbs me especially is that this numbing of the brain is something we share with the Chinese, who are subjected to it daily, hourly, every moment of their conscious lives. They cannot escape from it. In a few days we will be able to shake it off. We can escape from it, but they cannot. Ultimately, I think, this massive propaganda is self-defeating, because it prevents new ideas from arising, because it imprisons the young within rigid rules of conformity, and because it increases the power of the ever-present bureaucracy, those iron-faced men whom Mao Tse-tung regarded as enemies of the state. If only the hundred flowers were permitted to bloom, what a difference it would make! All the pent-up spiritual and intellectual resources of the Chinese people would be released and they would surge forward with renewed confidence and vigor!

We have not seen a single Chinese reading or holding the little red book during all our travels. It appears to have gone out of fashion. There are copies of the book in various languages including Finnish and Serbo-Croatian on wooden racks in hotels and airports: evidently for foreigners. We have seen none in the factories or schools. It has been revised several times since the day when there was an effusive introduction by Lin Piao. I suspect that it has outlived its usefulness and is now just one more of the documents which will be studied by scholars when they come to write a new history of the Chinese Communist party.

"Why don't you wear your Mao button?" the nearly pretty girl in the red stocking cap asked me this morning.

I shrugged my shoulders. Nearly everyone in the group wears the little red badge with Mao's profile stamped on it. It is made of very thin metal, Mao's profile is painted gold and bathed in a halo of thin rays, and down below, also in gold, there is a tiny picture of the Gate of Heavenly Peace in Peking. I have seen very few Chinese wearing the badge, and those who do wear it are usually the bureaucrats and the people in charge of factories.

"I don't like wearing badges," I said mildly.

"That means you are against the regime," she said in a loud voice full of indignation. "I don't know why they allowed you to come on the trip! You are against everything here! I know it!"

I said I didn't care a damn what she thought, I was not against the regime, and I didn't wear the button because I had met Mao and talked with him and when I knew him he did not look like a god with sun rays bursting out of his head. She murmured something and wandered away. All evening she has been watching me suspiciously, and I observe that she is now wearing two buttons, one on her stocking cap and one nicely balanced on the nipple of her left breast.

It may be the onset of senility, but I find myself increasingly infuriated by the handful of callow young Marxists on the trip who talk about China as though it was the Promised Land. How wonderful! There are no prostitutes, no taxes, no classes, no drunkards, no automobiles in private hands, no air pollution, no wealth, no poverty, the shops are full of consumer goods, and the millennium is within sight. I find this impossible to believe. I do not think Chou En-lai ever believed this. Air pollution? Shanghai's air pollution is very nearly as bad as New York's. As for taxes, there is an abundance of hidden taxes, and of course the communes are heavily taxed. No classes? But there is a managerial class so powerful, so conscious of its power, and so wealthy in comparison with the factory workers that it deserves to be called "the upper class," and the factory workers who earn thirty-five yuan a month obviously belong to "the lower class." Mao Tse-tung became bitterly disillusioned by the managers and the bureaucrats and launched the Great Proletarian Cultural Revolution against them. For a while the Red

Guards took over the country, arresting any bureaucrat who displeased them and executing summary judgment on them. The upheaval very nearly wrecked the country. Finally the Red Guards had to be rounded up and sent to work in the barren territories of the northwest because they were totally useless, dangerous, and anarchic. Today bureaucrats are often sent out to work in the fields for longer or shorter periods of time, and I regard this as a very healthy sign. But it seems to me that the Great Proletarian Cultural Revolution was an inadequate response to a serious problem.

We are incorrigible photographers. No sooner have we reached a factory than we go around madly searching for something to photograph. We are twenty-four Americans with about forty cameras between us. In the intervals of talking Marxism, the younger ones talk about their complicated and expensive equipment, the prices of new lenses, the secrets of the dark room. I have an Olympus bought for fifty dollars in Hong Kong, a Polaroid, and a small Japanese movie camera, so I am among the worst of them. Sometimes you can hear twenty-four shutters clacking at once. We are creatures with a herd instinct. If someone finds a good angle, we imitate him shamelessly. Someone once described our group erroneously as "twenty-four Americans searching for the Marxist way of life." This was nonsense. It would be more accurate to say that we are twenty-four American camera buffs let loose in a strange and beautiful country, intent only on wasting as much film as possible. We are camera-mad, and the Chinese look at our cameras with envy and astonishment.

Mao's handwriting. Mao is dead, but his handwriting is likely to endure. We see it everywhere, sometimes on silk, sometimes on huge billboards where the individual characters are carved out in wood and then gilded, and most often in black-and-white reproductions of his poems, the handwriting being vastly magnified. The poem most often reproduced is "The Long March," which he wrote in 1935. An enormous reproduction of the poem in gilded wood against a blood-red background gazes down at the traveler in the Canton airport:

> *The Red Army does not fear the trials*
> *   of the Long March.*
> *A thousand mountains and ten thousand*
> *   rivers are as nothing to them:*
> *The Five Ridges ripple like little waves,*
> *The peaks of Wu Meng roll by like mud balls.*
> *Warm are the cloud-topped cliffs washed*
> *   by the River of Golden Sand,*
> *Cold are the iron chains that span the*
> *   Tatu River.*
> *The myriad snows of the Min Mountain only*
> *   make them happier.*
> *The three Armies march on, every face glowing.*

I suppose he liked this poem best because it is full of the exultation of victory. It is surprising how often he exults in his poems. Later, when he grew older, the poems became like riddles with obscure meanings which can be interpreted in many different ways, and there is something oddly menacing about them, as though they were written in a secret language, but even in these poems there can sometimes be detected a note of exultation although it is not clear what victory he is celebrating. In his long lifetime he published only thirty-six poems, but it is likely that he wrote more than five hundred.

Mao Tse-tung as poet is something of a phenomenon. It was not uncommon for Chinese revolutionaries to write poems, and there are some memorable poems written by the revolutionaries who fought in the 1911 revolution against the Manchus. Ho Chi-minh wrote a cycle of prison poems, full of pity for his fellow prisoners. But Mao Tse-tung's poems are remarkable for their color and vigor, their springing eloquence, and heroic drama. He sees himself as a hero pitting himself against destiny, reaching toward great positions while fighting against unimaginably powerful enemies. It is intensely personal poetry, romantic to the highest degree, and like all romantic poetry it is self-regarding. The motive behind it is a powerful urge to dominate landscapes and peoples. If Napoleon had written poems, they would be like Mao Tse-tung's.

His calligraphy reflects his themes. It is always exuberant, urgent, a little florid, and very swift. Here, for example, are the words: *A single spark can start a prairie fire*. It is not, of course, an original thought—it derives from Lenin and before Lenin from Chernyshevsky. Mao Tse-tung shows the sparks blazing into a full-scale fire, and you can almost hear the roar of the undergrowth exploding into flames.

On the last line there is his signature written from left to right. It is fairly neat and controlled, unlike his usual signature which resembles a cascade of fireworks descending vertically.

An album of his calligraphy has been published in a massive volume. I was told that it was out of print, but finally found a copy in Shanghai, well bound in heavy paper of the familiar gunmetal-blue color and printed on excellent rice paper. The page is twelve inches by seventeen inches, which makes it technically, I believe, an elephant-sized book. Sometimes he writes with a heavy brush and the huge characters race across the page like galloping horses, and at other times, with a thinner brush, he moves with the intricate delicacy of a skater on a polished sheet of ice. It is not, I think, great calligraphy, and if you place it beside the great masters of calligraphy it appears to be lacking in real strength and true nobility. He had evidently studied calligraphy with care, and was influenced by the running script of the Northern Sung dynasty. There was a time when I admired his calligraphy inordinately on the basis of the few reproductions that were available. Now, with this huge collection in front of me, I am troubled by a certain theatricality and flamboyance. I like his calligraphy less and his poetry more.

They have told us that there is so little hotel space in China that we must all share rooms. Most of the time I have been sharing rooms with an Irishman of great charm and erudition, who worked in factories most of his life, fought the trade unions, joined the Communist party of America and was thrown out when he protested publicly against its hard anti-Maoist line. By profession he is a television repairman, which he describes as an ideal profession since he can choose his own hours. He snores prodigiously —last night his snoring was like the roar of a bull elephant. Most of the time I am rather deaf, but last night unfortunately I could hear the whole orchestra and every instrument. I am hoping that tonight I shall be a little deafer.

He is the only real Marxist among us, and I suspect that he is somewhat disillusioned. He cannot abide dogmatism and has no respect for bureaucrats, and we are surrounded by dogmas and bureaucrats. At the worst times he is wonderfully cheerful and he has the patience of Job. When this journey is over, I shall remember his crackling laughter and his gentleness.

I thought I knew a good deal about Mao Tse-tung's poetry, but this evening my Irish friend surprised me with a translation of a poem said to have been written by Mao in his old age. It reads:

> *The tiger averts his head,*
> *The tattered lion grieves,*
> *The bear flaunts its claws*
> *While riding the back of the cow,*
> *The moon torments the sun,*
> *The pagoda gives forth light,*
> *And disaster comes to birth*
> *While an olive branch is waving.*

Although the poem sounds in English like something out of Nostradamus, it is probably authentic Mao. The code can be unscrambled fairly easily. *Tiger* = United States. *Lion* = Britain. *Bear* = Soviet Union. *Cow* = India. *Pagoda* = Vietnam. All this makes a kind of poetic sense, and in addition there is the fact that Mao enjoyed wearing his prophetic robes. My friend cannot remember where he first encountered the poem.

Occasionally we have meetings to discuss our itinerary and all the problems of journeying through China. These meetings are mostly a waste of time, those who enjoy speaking speak at enormous length, and in any case our itinerary has been decided in Peking and the problems of journeying through China are numerous and insoluble.

We are all blinded by the fame and magnificence of Peking, and we want to go there as quickly as possible. According to the itinerary we shall go to Tsinan and Tsingtao, which mean very little to us. Tsinan is the capital of Shantung province, Tsingtao is a great naval base and a former German colony. We argue that if we could avoid going to Tsinan and/or Tsingtao, we would have much more time in Peking. We hear from the guides that telegrams have been dispatched to Peking explaining our "point of view." In fact we have no point of view: merely a forlorn hope. We would be wildly happy to have ten days in Peking, and we care very little about Tsinan and Tsingtao, where we shall spend a week.

So the debate continues between the handful of diehard Marxists and the rest. The diehard Marxists say that we are the guests of the country, that the guides know best, and that it is impolite and impolitic to ask them to grant us special favors. The theme that papa knows best was therefore repeated ad nauseam. The opposition countered with the argument that we were on a friendship tour and that friendship should work both ways. There were other arguments: we had not been consulted about the itinerary. Why not? We were not people who could be casually moved across a chessboard at someone's whim. There should be free discussions with the guides, all opinions should be taken into account, and the majority should decide. The arguments were not heated, but there was an underlying bitterness. The diehard Marxists were obviously in favor of Obedience to Authority, and the rest of us wanted Freedom. The battle between the great abstractions was joined.

Like all the other members of the loyal opposition, I am hoping against hope that we shall take the train to Peking and avoid Tsinan and Tsingtao.

TSINAN

The Fountains and the Streams

It is easy to imagine a man in some distant province of China saying that he will sell all his goods and go on pilgrimage to Peking. We tell ourselves that Peking is the place of splendor, the fiercely glamorous city, the one place that has the power to cast a spell on men's souls. We can hardly imagine that he would sell his goods in order to make a pilgrimage to a place called Tsinan in Shantung province. Tsinan, we tell ourselves, has no glamour, no resonance. We have heard very little about it: therefore it cannot be very important. In fact, throughout Chinese history, more people have gone on pilgrimage to Tsinan than to any other city. Not far from Tsinan is Tai Shan, the Holy Mountain, reverenced by the Chinese since time immemorial. In this province too are the birthplaces of the great Chinese philosophers Confucius and Mencius. To a very large extent Chinese civilization begins here.

The Chinese say they can recognize a man from Shantung half a mile away. He has a distinctive walk, a rather lean bony frame, a quick intelligence, and an air of accomplishment; he is taller than the Chinese of the south, but not so tall nor so heavy boned as the people of Peking. From Shantung come beautiful women, philosophers, chefs, engineers, sailors, and actors. They regard themselves as people of the center, neither as placid as the northerners nor as excitable as the southerners, having the best of both worlds.

They say, too, that in Tsinan you have only to push a stick into the earth and a fountain will gush out. Pleasant streams shaded by willows run through the city, fed by fountains that pour out of strange rocks resembling blocks of lava from an ancient volcano. These rocks are pale white or pale gray, with as many air holes as a sponge, and the Chinese through the centuries have amused themselves by setting them alongside the streams or by building clusters of them in rock gardens. All the springs feed into the lake known as the Ta Ming or Great Brightness Lake, which is very nearly as beautiful as the West Lake in Hangchow. We went out on the lake on a day when there was a light mist and the willow-shaded islands seemed to be swimming toward us like islands in a dream, and all round the lake there were temples converted into museums and exhibition halls. Here and there to the north of the lake the water was frozen over, and the fallen willow leaves and the dead lotuses caught in the ice produced patterns of desolation, while on the lakeshore the red-pillared pavilions flaunted their magnificence.

Tsinan was civilized, ebullient, aware of its ancient history, exulting in its sweet-water springs. There was a time when many of these springs were fed into ornamental pools in private gardens. The Chinese Communists very sensibly tore down the walls between the gardens and made a great park that betrays its original character: a park made out of many parks. Here are pavilions, painted kiosks, ancient temples, ornamental bridges, intricately carved marble railings, long avenues of ancient trees, rest houses where you can take shelter from the sun, tea houses where you can drink green tea brewed with water from these fountains. There are no loudspeakers blaring martial music; no street noises penetrate these gardens. The park made out of many parks gives an impression of the utmost luxuriance.

And suddenly you come upon something which is totally unexpected—a pool with a gleaming white marble balustrade, which resembles many other pools except that it is boiling over, the surface erupting with those small, sharp, insistent waves that you see when water is boiling. You find yourself thinking: "It is perfectly all right. Why shouldn't a pool boil over? There is no law that says the surface of a pool must be flat." But, of course, there is such a law, and you find yourself a little puzzled, even a little disturbed. Why should the laws of nature be held in abeyance? Deep down in the black waters of the boiling pool a red sea lion—at least the Chinese call it a sea lion, though it resembles a dolphin—is racing from one end of the pool to the other and back again, rarely rising to the surface. The pool is perhaps twenty feet long, the sea lion is four or five feet. He has solved the problem of perpetual motion. He races back and forth like a red tiger in a cage.

The Chinese children bend double over the marble railings and peer into the depths of the pool, enchanted by the mysterious creature who is scarcely more than a red shadow moving disconcertingly in the black waters, vanishing, reappearing, vanishing again, behaving exactly as dragons may be expected to behave. The Chinese have an inordinate affection for this boiling pool. The trick has been accomplished by the flow of three separate springs moving at different speeds and at different levels. Mathematics and hydraulics have been placed in the service of human enjoyment.

Tsinan is full of these delights. We came at dusk to the Provincial Shantung Museum, housed in an old palace, red-pillared, double-roofed, a place of great dignity. The ancient bronzes, the Han figurines, the Tang wall paintings found in nearby tombs, the swords and halberds and chariot fittings, and the armies of wooden soldiers from the Ming dynasty were all finely displayed. In the Red Pagoda at Canton we saw a museum where the objects were so ill-displayed that it was impossible to believe that the museum director cared about them. In Tsinan the museum director evidently cared very deeply. Room after room opened out to reveal the treasures of Shantung—not too many, but enough to whet the appetite. To the east of Tsinan there are sites dating from the great age of Shang: bronze vessels of great magnificence therefore occupied pride of place, gleaming with a rich apple-green patina. There were about a hundred bronze swords, also dating from the Shang dynasty; they too had rusted into a wonderfully rich green color. Then there were bronze drums and bronze musical bells, dating from about 1500 B.C. The room where they were gathered quivered with the power of the Shang emperors.

Although the emperors of the Han dynasty were perhaps even more powerful, for they ruled over a vastly larger empire, their arts were more humble and more human. The abstract gods represented in bronze gave way to representations of human figures, so we have a large number of pottery figurines of men, women, children, and the animals that could be found in the house. These figurines are not especially graceful; they are rugged, heavy, earthy. The Shantung museum has a famous group of dancers, musicians, and acrobats found in 1969 near Tsinan. None of the figures is more than three inches high. One beats a drum, two others are turning somersaults, others play on flutes, and the rest dance, the men on one side and the women on the other. They are robust, healthy people, and we have no doubt they will bump into one another and think nothing of it. These pottery figures are brightly colored and the breath of life flows through them.

It was the same throughout this small and exquisite museum. The setting was exactly right—in China an old palace serves admirably to display the treasures of the past. A modern museum, all white walls and neon lighting, would destroy these objects by giving them a totally meaningless setting. They needed the proportions of a Chinese room; they needed the folding doors and the flaring eaves and the high roof. In the simplest possible way, by using what was at hand, the museum director had solved the problem of building the perfect museum.

We had argued against visiting Tsinan, saying that we wanted above all to spend more time in Peking. Now that we were in Tsinan, we wanted to see more of it and more of the surrounding region. Mount Tai, the Holy Mountain, especially attracted us. Chufu, the birthplace of Confucius, was within reach. It appeared that Shantung was the ancient state of Lu, which once possessed formidable armies and formidable philosophers. Out of this province came many of the men who forged Chinese civilization. Our guides looked at us darkly when we mentioned Confucius. He was being attacked vociferously in the Chinese press. The Chinese Communists had recently taken up the position that Confucius was the source of all evil, strangely coupling his name with Lin Piao, the general who until recently had been Mao Tse-tung's chosen successor. "Down with Confucius and Lin Piao" was the slogan that had appeared on all the walls of China before the new slogan was invented: "Down with the Gang of Four." We reminded the guides that even if Confucius was in ill-favor, he was a giant whose shadow fell over Chinese history and we would be pleased to pay our respects to him in his birthplace. If we had gone to Hunan, we would have been pleased to pay our respects to the birthplace of Mao Tse-tung.

The guides however were very firm. Confucius was in disgrace. He was the enemy of China, the running dog of feudalism, the perverter of Chinese morality. They were quite sure that the authorities in Peking would look askance at our request. A visit to Tai Shan was another matter; it could perhaps be justified by its historical significance, and if we were insistent they would take it up with Peking. "But why," one of the guides asked, "are you so interested in early Chinese history? It has no importance at all."

So it happened that the entire group of twenty-four Americans met in the dimly lit reception room in the hotel in Tsinan to discuss whether or not we should seek permission to visit the Holy Mountain. It fell to me to make the presentation, telling the story of the mountain that had been venerated since the beginning of Chinese civilization. Here the ancient emperors had prayed to heaven on behalf of the people, worshiping alone on the highest rock of the mountain that was believed to be the earthly equivalent of the Pole Star, firm, unchangeable, beautiful, and here countless temples were erected in honor of the ancient gods. Out of twenty-four, twenty-three of us voted to go to Tai Shan. On the following day we were told: "It is out of the question. We must follow the plan that has already been approved in Peking."

The Buddhas on the Cliffs

On one of those pure blue mornings when the sky seems infinitely high and the Chinese mountains seem to be dancing, we set out from Tsinan to see a hospital deep in the countryside. It was a very special kind of hospital, for it served many villages and hamlets for many miles around and was a training center for barefoot doctors. We were happy to go there, for whenever we visited a hospital or a clinic in China we were aware of the warm breath of humanity, of kindness and gentleness. The doctors and nurses were dedicated. In the hospitals and clinics there was very little propaganda, and though the obligatory portrait of Mao Tse-tung hung on the walls of some rooms, it was not in every room. "Serve the people," he had said, and here they were well served.

With one or two exceptions all the doctors we saw in China were quiet and reserved, possessing a Buddha-like calm, content with themselves and their work. We could recognize a party bureaucrat at twenty paces: hard, ambitious, conscious of his place in society, always talking in jargon and therefore unthinkingly. He saw himself as a figure of power and authority, and was usually better dressed than the people around him. No doubt in a communist society there must be bosses; they must be paid more than the others; they must have the means to exert their authority. But Mao Tse-tung had recognized long ago that these tough, hard-headed bureaucrats were very dangerous to the revolution. "They are eight-sided and slippery as eels," he wrote. "They beat their gongs to blaze the way. They cause people to be afraid just by looking at them." We saw more of these bureaucrats than we wanted to see, and it was obvious almost from the first day we were in China that they now occupy the places once occupied by the feudal lords, magistrates, and overseers of an earlier age.

So we were happy once more to be among doctors, and were not disappointed. They were quiet, methodical, good-looking people who lived in a building that resembled a low-walled fortress in the shadow of mountains, with two large courtyards, with the offices and laboratories set against the outer walls, all of them quite small and primitive but scrupulously clean. It was called the Liu Pu People's Commune and served some fifty thousand people in this remote mountainous region. There were only fifty-nine workers in the hospital, including doctors and nurses, but this figure did not include the many barefoot doctors who kept close contact with the hospital while they made their rounds in the villages. Altogether there were sixty-six barefoot doctors attached in this way to the hospital staff. In the past there were very few doctors in this region; they charged exorbitant fees, and the peasants, who could rarely afford the fees, avoided the doctors until they were *in extremis*. Black fever was rampant, while smallpox, diphtheria, and measles carried away hundreds of children every year. Meningitis was also prevalent.

"We came here first in 1952," the doctor was saying. "The aim was to eliminate the major diseases as rapidly as possible, but in those days we had no hospital—this was built six years later. We went to every village, inoculating everyone, keeping records, teaching the peasants about sanitation, doing whatever could be done with a very small staff. Then we realized that we simply had to have a hospital, and the work became much better organized and we gradually built up an organization of barefoot doctors. This hospital is a kind of halfway house. We still send difficult cases to Tsinan. We are not equipped like the big hospitals, although we have an X-ray machine, microscopes, an operating theater, laboratories, a dispensary. We work here on the middle level between the barefoot doctors who go into people's houses and the well-equipped city hospitals. We mend broken bones and cure diseases which are not too troublesome and respond to drugs. We are the guardians of health in this community. We are not brilliant surgeons. We are very ordinary."

So they were, and it was precisely their ordinariness that was so appealing. The doctors spoke gravely about their difficulties—they did not always have the equipment or the drugs they needed. The floors were brick; the small rooms were bare, rather bleak, and there were only a few small charcoal fires to take away the sting of the bitter cold. In these regions the temperature varies from $-4°$ to $120°$, and while I huddled round the iron stove, warming myself back to life and wondering why my fingers were so numb, I was sure it was $-4°$. Outside, the sky was a wonderfully clear icy blue.

I found myself wondering why this plain, simple hospital set down in the middle of nowhere was so deeply moving. Perhaps it was because the devotion and dedication of the doctors was something that could be felt, or perhaps it was precisely because everything was so simple and so primitive. And then it occurred to me that this was the closest thing in China to a monastery in an age when there were no more working monasteries, no more Buddhist priests; for after the Cultural Revolution the Buddhist priesthood was dissolved, or if not completely dissolved, then reduced to such insignificance that it no longer possessed any influence on the Chinese people. These doctors performed a sacramental office. They were the priests of a new dispensation, the servants of the servants, the solitary remnants of an ancient tradition of service. "Serve the people?" Yes, a hundred times yes! But it seemed to me that the doctors served the people to the uttermost, while the bureaucrats and the party bosses served the people only when it suited their purpose.

"We work day and night, and never rest," one of the doctors said, and it was easy to believe him.

About a quarter of the people in our group were suffering from heavy colds. We were wheezing, sneezing, coughing, shivering, choking. Some of us were coughing so violently that we resembled puppets jerking on strings. Deciding that something had to be done about this as soon as possible or we would be dead before evening, we advanced on the dispensary in search of medicines, followed by one of our official guides, a small impatient woman who would have preferred us simply to fall into a single line behind her. She said there wasn't time to go to the dispensary. A visit to the dispensary was apparently not on the itinerary, and therefore could not be contemplated. When we crowded into the dispensary, she attempted to wave us away.

"Too many people!" she shouted. "Get them tomorrow! Get them some other day!"

"We all have bad colds today," someone said.

"Doesn't matter! Get them some other day!" And a moment later she was shouting: "Too many people! Too many people!" as though these words, having lodged in her brain, had acquired the quality of an incantation, the magic spell that would make us vanish.

We were given aspirins for our colds and tetracycline for our coughs, and left the dispensary in triumph. The drugs cost only a few fen and were about one-twentieth the price they would have been at home. By this time our guide looked angry, and I was angrier. Some time later, when we were in the bus traveling away from the hospital, it occurred to me that I should be grateful to her, for she had supplied an essential clue to the nature of those who order our lives, the bureaucrats, the bosses, the bigots who make life intolerable for so many people all over the world, not only in Communist China. "Too many people!" she cried impatiently, scarcely realizing that she was repeating the battle cry of bureaucrats everywhere.

About fifteen minutes later, after climbing a steep winding road, we came to an enchanted valley set among mountains shaped like curling waves. This high valley was the site of a Buddhist monastery that dated back to the sixth century A.D. and was at the height of its power and influence during the Sung dynasty. All we knew at the time was that we were being taken to the Thousand Buddha Cliffs. We did not know that we would soon be seeing some of the supreme achievements of Chinese sculpture.

Even in winter the horseshoe-shaped valley remained green and luxuriant. There were streams nearby, the wind had dropped, it grew warmer, and it was very pleasant to wander along a narrow pathway to the Thousand Buddha Cliffs, past a brilliantly painted kiosk that had evidently been painted only a few months before and was the mirror image of another kiosk on the other side of the valley. A Chinese kiosk can be very elaborate, and these were among the most elaborate I had ever seen. And then quite suddenly we were in the shadow of the cliffs with the thousand Buddhas carved on them—perhaps not a thousand, for I counted barely a hundred, but there were many others higher up on the cliff wall and farther along the valley. The cliff was alive with Buddhas of all periods, some of them by good sculptors, while others were carved so inexpertly that one wondered how they could have been permitted to find a place here. Some were a few inches high, others were five or six feet high; and there were a few that seemed to be unfinished, as though the sculptors had been at work when they were overcome by invaders. But what was especially notable about the cliff wall was the sense of crowded, pulsating life, even though the Buddhas were nearly always in the same attitude of blessing, silent and remote from the world. The sculptors, by filling every cranny of the cliff, by carving in many different styles over many centuries, had given movement to the figure of Buddha. A single Buddha carved on the cliff would lead you inward into the rock, while a hundred Buddhas, all insisting on their presence, lead you out of the rock into the teeming, bustling world of activity, of human hopes and human despairs. In this way the rock face became a spectacle, a procession, a ceremony, and all this had come about because the people wanted spectacles, processions, and ceremonies rather than the portrait of Buddha withdrawn from the world.

On that narrow ledge, in the shadow of the overhanging pine trees, there were lessons to be learned about the nature of Chinese Buddhist art. Superb carvings were at ease beside journeyman work; the carvings of different periods were at ease with one another; the rough was at ease with the smooth. The greater and more finished works stood out, but there was a sense of the community of Buddha through time and space. The ill-carved, squat, and ugly Buddha had just as much right to be there as the finished and perfected work. The cliff resembled an enormous curtain displaying the innumerable faces of Buddha, which were all the same face and at the same time all wonderfully different because they were carved at different periods and under different dispensations.

I had never seen a rock face carved with Buddhas before, although I had seen many photographs. But even the best photographs were unable to suggest the texture of the rock, the way it was veined and seamed, and how the sculptors had taken advantage of veins and seams. Photographs fail, too, to convey the texture and structure of landscapes. This horseshoe-shaped valley was a very complex and beautiful thing, with many levels, many wandering pathways, many avenues, and many balconies. Indeed, the whole valley was theatrical and the strangely shaped mountains high above us only made it more theatrical. The Buddhist priests who once lived here had evidently land-scaped the valley. Thus, about a hundred feet below the cliff wall, they had leveled off an area about the size of two football fields to serve as a platform for a forest of pagodas made of stone and brick, a few carved sumptu-ously and others quite plain. These pagodas were the reliquaries of the chief abbots who once ruled over the immense valley.

This platform resembled a garden, and I imagined a time when flowers grew there and the yellow pagodas were only the tallest and most beautiful of the flowers. Every-thing about this place suggested an effortless good taste. For more than thirteen hundred years, perhaps longer, the Buddhist monks had cultivated this valley, shaped it, planted it, built little pavilions and rest houses where they were needed, and so made it their own. Now not a single Buddhist monk remained.

We walked across a stone bridge and came to another brilliantly painted kiosk. A few yards farther on we saw a small square building with a hipped roof surmounted by a tiny golden pagoda formed of many rings. The building stood on a yellow bluff overlooking the widening valley. Four doors were cut into it. The proportions of the doors were wonderfully calculated to balance the proportions of the roof. Inside, set on high pedestals, were four marble Buddhas of great simplicity and great beauty. They were the Buddhas of the Four Directions, whose purpose was to protect and bless all living creatures. The art historian Osvald Sirén, who visited this temple in 1922, concluded that these Buddhas were carved in the Northern Ch'i dynasty about 544 A.D. He also concluded that the Four Gate Temple was the oldest surviving stone building in China.

The Yellow River

About three miles north of Tsinan, the Yellow River, the curse of China, makes a bend on its long journey to the sea. Because it was so close to the city there were some of us who felt we should be given an opportunity to see it. Our guides were adamant. "It's just a river like any other," they told us. "We haven't time." We had spent a good deal of time visiting factories and listening to the propaganda speeches of the factory bosses, and for once we felt we had a good argument. We intended to see the Yellow River even if it meant walking there, for we knew that it had played an important and devastating role in Chinese history. We, too, could be adamant.

While our guides insisted that all rivers look alike, we maintained that all rivers were different and the Yellow River was particularly different. How many rivers had overflowed their banks and drowned whole provinces? Also, the Chinese Communist engineers had finally tamed it, an achievement greatly to their credit. We affirmed our desire to pay our respects to the engineers, and they hinted that the river was a military area. We said: "You would not let us see Mount Tai, which is forty miles away. Surely you can let us see the Yellow River, which is less than four miles away." Finally we were permitted to see the river, although it was not on the itinerary. I suspect that they called the governor of the province, the mayor of Tsinan, and the Army Corps of Engineers before we were permitted to make the three-mile journey. It was a hard-fought battle, but we won it. We did not win many battles.

The Yellow River is not one of those beautiful rivers like the Hudson and the St. Lawrence which captivate you because they are mirrors for spectacular landscapes. The poets have rarely celebrated it, and until recently the

laboring people have always cursed it because it overflowed its banks, changed course, and caused more havoc
than any river has a right to do. But today it is tamed, and
very quiet. We were still in the suburbs of Tsinan when
we saw what appeared to be a low hill in front of us. The
bus roared up to the crest of the hill, and there was the
Yellow River in front of us, about half a mile wide, lying
comfortably within its high stone banks, like a blue lake.
The river with the sinister reputation was about fifteen
feet deep, with yellow sandbanks emerging at intervals.
Far in the distance a craggy mountain, steel-blue in the
morning light, served as the solitary guardian of an immense gleaming plain. Children were playing along the
shore. There was no traffic on the river until at last three
long barges, roped together and pushed by a tugboat,
emerged from the bend of the river and solemnly moved
downstream like ships in a dream.

One of the guides was telling us that the river proved
the advantages of Chinese communism, for only the Communists had succeeded in taming it. This was not quite
true, for it had been tamed many times. She went on to
describe how Chiang Kai-shek had once given orders to
breach the dikes, so that the river overflowed and drowned
a quarter of a million peasants. This was one more example
of the hideous propensity of the former feudal government
to act irresponsibly toward the peasantry. She forgot to
say that the dikes were breached in order to prevent the
Japanese army from advancing, and the tragic decision
was forced upon him. By dynamiting the embankments
of the swollen river at Chengchow, he drowned many
thousands of Japanese and rendered useless their artillery
and motorized units, and so delayed the capture of Hankow
by three months. No one knows how many thousands of
Chinese peasants were drowned.

The guides were always telling us how terrible and
ruthless the former feudal government had been, but they
seemed to know very little about it. In their eyes China
came to birth in 1949, and all its history was a waiting for
Mao Tse-tung. As for Chinese literature, they seemed to
know nothing at all. I asked them whether they had read
the great poet Li Tai Po, and they said he was decadent,
and of Su Tung Po that he was merely a feudal official
in a dissolute court. They had a grudging respect for Tu Fu,
which is like having a grudging respect for Shakespeare.
They had not read his works, but regarded him as one of
those who were "for the people."

This puzzled me, for when I was teaching in China, my
students knew hundreds of pages of the great Chinese
poets by heart. They regarded the poets as a part, and the
greater part, of the heritage of Chinese culture. Our guides
could recite the poems of Mao Tse-tung, but their knowledge of Chinese poetry ended with him. In the old days
students trained their memories, while the present-day
students seemed to have no memory at all.

For a long time we gazed at the Yellow River flowing
below us without a ripple or a shadow to mar its beauty,
so slow a river that it seemed capable of moving backward
slowly and inexorably toward the distant Kunlun Mountains far away in the west, where it has its source.

Maple Tree Village

When we arrived at the cinema a huge crowd had formed.
We thought at first they were waiting to see the film but
then we realized they were waiting to see us—twenty-four
rather shabby and exhausted Americans who had seen
many factories and schools that day and would go on to

see more factories and schools the following day. They were good-humored, curious, not demonstrative; they smiled and waved a little; we smiled and waved back with an odd feeling that we scarcely deserved their attentions but wished we could sit down and talk with them.

We were given the best seats in the front rows of the balcony. The house was packed, the audience was quiet and attentive, the film which came on immediately after we were seated was in brightest Technicolor. *Maple Tree Village* was about an uprising in a small mountainous village. The enemy was a feudal landlord who owned the villagers body and soul and looked like a crafty fox, while nearly all the villagers were young and handsome, with rosy cheeks. The leader of the uprising was a sleek young man brimming with good health, well fed, very sure of himself. He looked indeed like a matinee idol from a musical comedy and was woefully miscast as the leader of a peasant insurrection, just as the feudal landlord was woefully miscast, being so evidently weak-willed and ineffective that it was inconceivable that he would present any real opposition to the peasants. From the beginning the peasants were bound to win. There was no conflict.

The young peasant leader had clearly studied the Peking opera. His gestures were always theatrical. Feet apart, chest distended, hands on hips, he addressed his followers with the air of a prophet addressing the Children of Israel, promising them a land full of milk and honey if only they would attack the landlord and his armed guards, who were dressed in black and equipped with Mausers. The guards looked like men of straw, who would surrender at the first opportunity. We saw them whispering together in the shadowy yamen, rolling their eyes, fondling their guns, making secret signs to one another as they prepare to quell the rebellion. They were caricatures of evil like the black-visaged demons of the Peking opera. And when the up-rising at last broke out, they ran around like maddened insects, shooting in all directions, displaying their incompetence as though they were proud of it. The revolutionaries had no difficulty capturing the landlord's palatial yamen. The landlord himself was arrested. Trussed up like a chicken, he was given a public trial and sentenced to death by the peasants, who were delirious with happiness for having rid themselves of their hated oppressor. A few moments later we saw a long column of heavily armed Kuomintang troops marching along mountain pathways. It was a formidable army, and the moment we set eyes on it we knew that the peasant rebellion was doomed. There followed on the wide screen a brilliant shot of a forest in autumn with red and orange leaves dancing boisterously in the high wind. It was the one memorable passage in the chaotic film, for the autumn leaves signified Mao Tse-tung's ill-fated Autumn Uprising of 1927. For almost a minute we gazed at the tossing leaves, while the voice of the commentator was saying: "There were many more defeats, but in the end came victory."

Maple Tree Village might have been a good film if it had been shot on location with a more believable cast. The story was essentially true; such uprisings did take place; and they were brutally put down. But it is impossibly difficult to produce on a Shanghai sound stage the feeling of an uprising, especially with actors who are continually mimicking the gestures of Peking opera. What the film lacked above all was verisimilitude. There was never a moment when we believed that a real uprising was taking place.

On another day we saw a film called *Pioneers*, which has some historical significance because it appears to have brought about the only recorded quarrel between Mao

Tse-tung and Chiang Ching, whose activities as chief censor were reducing the Chinese film industry to a state of frenzy. She reportedly refused four times to see the film. When finally the film was shown to her in a private screening, she showed an intense dislike for it. Halfway through the film she fell into a rage and demanded loudly to know who was being praised. Although Chou En-lai was not named, she insisted that the film, which was about the Taching oil field in northeastern China, was really a disguised attempt to celebrate the accomplishments of Chou En-lai over the accomplishments of her husband. Accordingly the film was banned. This was not quite the end of the matter, for the resourceful film director succeeded in setting up a private screening of the film for Mao Tse-tung, who said: "There is no big error in the film. It is not necessary to nitpick." But even though Mao Tse-tung had given his approval, the ban on the film remained. The film was not shown publicly until November 1976, after Chiang Ching's arrest.

Once again there is a handsome matinee-idol hero, an oil engineer seeking to discover oil in a harsh and uninhabited region of China. At first he has no success, partly because saboteurs have infiltrated the group but also because there is no oil in the place where the oil rigs have been set up. Things are going very badly when it occurs to the hero that all his problems will be solved if he studies Mao Tse-tung's little red book, and so for perhaps half a minute we see him, with deeply furrowed brows, bent over the book. Gradually the furrows are smoothed out, the light of certainty shines in his eyes, and he bounds across the room to order the workmen to haul down the derricks and move them to another spot in the trackless desert. It is generally assumed that this scene was inserted into the movie at the orders of Chiang Ching. We see the gear being hauled down. A storm arises, and we see the workmen carrying it away in the teeth of the storm. When we see the derricks again, they have been put up in exactly the right spot. Oil gushes out, the workmen are jubilant, there is the feeling that their enormous toil is being rewarded. The hero, however, has a hunch that all is not going well. He returns to his office just in time to see one of his closest advisers pouring oil on a piece of matting. In this way we learn that there are saboteurs in the highest places, for it is clear that the man was about to throw flaming matting in the direction of the gusher. The hero shoots the saboteur just in time. While an invisible orchestra plays "The Song of Mao Tse-tung" the camera returns to the joyful faces of the workmen as they watch the oil pouring out of the good earth.

Like *Maple Tree Village* this film is disturbing because there is never a moment when we feel we are in the presence of reality. It is highly operatic, the gestures are always obvious, the matinee idol is always at the center of the stage. The derrick is obviously made of pasteboard and except for a few location shots the entire film appears to have been made in the Shanghai studios. For once Chiang Ching was quite right: the film deserved to be banned.

After the Russian Revolution there emerged an extraordinary group of young film-makers who seemed to be charged with the energy of the revolution. Eisenstein, Pudovkin, Dziga Vertov, and many others made memorable films which can be studied with pleasure fifty years after they were made, and no doubt they will still be studied in a hundred years' time. They distorted and falsified Russian history, for they were propagandists under orders to present the Communists in the best light. Nicholas II and Alexander Kerensky are presented as buffoons, as Chiang

Kai-shek and his lieutenants are presented as buffoons in Chinese films. But the Soviet films possessed a passionate vitality, a sense of swift movement, a deep feeling for the grandeur of history. *Earth, The End of St. Petersburg, Chapayev, Storm over Asia* were masterpieces. In twenty-seven years the Chinese Communist film-makers have produced nothing to equal them. Why? We are told that it is all the fault of Chiang Ching. I suspect that the real reason goes deeper, that not only Chiang Ching but the entire bureaucracy was lacking in film sense and imagination. Why was no film made of the Long March? We hear of quarrels in the higher echelons of the party, of a film half-finished and then abandoned, of film directors who were arrested and vanished from sight. The Long March was the single most powerful legend created by the Chinese Communists and cried out to be made into a powerful film, and now it may be too late, for scarcely anyone who took part in it remains alive.

After seeing *Maple Tree Village* we went out into the quiet night of Tsinan. The crowd that came to see us enter the cinema had returned to watch us again, silent, undemonstrative, good-humored, very curious. The air was sweet and pure, as befitted a city of streams and fountains, and the moon was riding high in a sky of broken clouds. Someone said a storm was coming—it was the first weather news we had heard since we left Hong Kong. And that night we took the train for Tsingtao, many miles to the east, and so we outreached the storm.

TSINGTAO

A Ghostly Church

When we came to Tsingtao, we knew nothing about the place except that it was a seaside resort which had once been a German enclave in China. We had not particularly wanted to go there and would have much preferred to go directly from Tsinan to Peking. It was winter, too cold to go bathing; the city possessed no outstanding monuments and had played no especially important role in Chinese history. We told ourselves that Tsingtao was a nuisance, and we could have spent our days far more profitably in Peking. The guides were adamant; the itinerary had been worked out and could not be changed.

We arrived in Tsingtao early in the morning when it was still dark, after a long journey by train. The train was uncomfortable, with very narrow bunks, and looked as though it had been made at the turn of the century. Very few of us were able to sleep, and we arrived at a hotel on the waterfront in various stages of exhaustion, hungry, disheveled, and out of temper, many of us still suffering from the heavy colds we acquired in Shaohsing, with running noses and hacking coughs. We looked more like refugees than privileged travelers. Someone said: "What in God's name are we doing in Tsingtao?" The question remained unanswered. The guides professed to be perplexed, wondering why we were so resentful.

In that damp, chilly early morning while we coughed up the yellow bile from our lungs and watched the sea mist thickening, the conviction that we had not the faintest interest in former German enclaves in China only increased. Meanwhile it would have to be endured.

In fact, Tsingtao was memorable precisely because the Germans had once taken possession of it, leaving on it a mark that the Chinese had not troubled to efface. Tsingtao was very strange indeed. We would see Germany transported to the Yellow Sea.

But during this early morning while our eyes were clogged with sleep and a white fog covered the sea, there was absolutely nothing to be seen. Tsingtao vanished. We looked out of the hotel window and saw nothing except the very faint shape of a Chinese pavilion that appeared to be hovering half a mile away, suspended over the sea. The pavilion was wonderfully shaped with pillars and a flaring roof but was no more than a silhouette painted on the fog, very frail and delicate, like one of those pavilions set on high crags in Chinese paintings. This seagoing pavilion made no sense. Obviously it was some kind of mirage. Obviously pavilions do not go out to sea.

At intervals we would go to the window and watch the ghostly apparition of this most enchanting and inexplicable pavilion, the shadow written on the fog. Sometimes it vanished altogether, at other times it acquired depth and substance while still appearing to be floating on the sea. We came to the conclusion that the pavilion was probably on an island which was bathed in fog. Half an hour later, while we were still looking at it, the fog melted away, and we saw at last that the pavilion was well anchored at the end of a long causeway and the flaring roof was bright yellow, like the roofs of the palaces in Peking. Far away lay the green islands that appeared to encircle the wide bay.

I rushed out to see the yellow pavilion. There was a cold wind, the tide was out, the sea was sparkling, all the islands around the bay were glowing in the morning light. It seemed to me that the pavilion was a staggering invention; it was exactly right and possessed the dimensions of a perfect work of art. Just as a pagoda set on a hill dominates a landscape, so that all the hills and valleys seem to be wheeling around it, so this small pavilion at the end of a causeway seemed to knit the whole landscape together, to provide a focus and a scale of measurement. I thought: if they had placed the pavilion twenty feet farther out to sea, it would have been hopelessly wrong. They knew exactly where to place it, almost to a hairbreadth.

By this time, although it was still early in the morning, a surprisingly large number of people were walking beside the sea wall. They were Red Army men taking an early morning stroll, children making their way to school, workmen on their way to the factories. What was more astonishing was the number of people walking vigorously along the causeway to the pavilion and back again, having no reason to do so except to enjoy the sun and the scenery. About eight people could walk abreast on the causeway, which was already crowded. There were no loudspeakers reciting the works of Mao Tse-tung, no military music was being played, no one was telling anyone else what to do. Paradise was a causeway and an elegant pavilion with a yellow roof. In fact, the roof on closer acquaintance turned out to be a rather ugly orange color, which the sun endowed with a massive and imperial brilliance.

Everything about the journey to the pavilion was exciting. The crowded causeway, the ketch that was putting out to sea, the line of sampans trailing one another like geese, the floating kelp beds which for some mysterious reason were being sprayed with water from a small ship that frisked about like a happy kitten, the deep blue of the waters, the sound of the sea slapping against the causeway. The islands and the sea were still wheeling gaily around the pavilion.

And then, as we returned along the causeway, looking at the shoreline of Tsingtao, there was another surprise awaiting us. All along the coast there were heavy Germanic buildings with overhanging roofs and dormer windows totally unlike any other buildings we had seen in China. They resembled baronial mansions. They must have been erected during the German occupation, which lasted from 1899 to 1914, and they had survived the subsequent Japanese occupation only because they had been built so solidly and so heavily that it would have taken many tons of dynamite to destroy them. Beyond them, riding high on a hill overlooking the bay, there was something even stranger, a huge white church with two enormous steeples, which seemed, at this distance, to be the size of the cathedral of Chartres or even larger. It gleamed in the sunlight, dominating the city, insolent and majestic, and looked as though it had been built only a few years ago, not at the beginning of the century.

The ghostly church riding over the Chinese city seemed unreal, irrelevant, absurd. Yet in its shape it possessed great beauty, and the bone-whiteness of the stone gave it a ghostly splendor. Although utterly unsuited to the Chinese landscape, it was nevertheless worthy of its Western architects. We learned later that the Chinese had converted it into a warehouse.

Today, when I think of Tsingtao, I remember the small pavilion at the end of the causeway, which differed scarcely at all from pavilions built two thousand years ago, and the white Gothic church rising serenely above the city, which differed scarcely at all from churches built in Europe seven hundred years ago, and they seem to be polar opposites, defying one another and yet at ease with one another, and there is a kind of harmony between them.

The Tunnels

All over China the earth has been honeycombed with tunnels designed to safeguard the population from atomic bombs. Hundreds of thousands, perhaps millions of people were employed in digging them. We were told that in Tsingtao there had been a call to arms and every available workingman was inducted into the work-gangs. For many years the tunneling went on, but now at last it was finished, though it was possible that there would be some further refinements. Since Tsingtao was a large industrial town and also a naval base, it was expected that it would be one of the first towns to be attacked.

In Tsingtao and later in Peking the Chinese spoke of atomic bombs in a matter-of-fact way, as though they were something inevitable, to be expected, not to be feared. I found their attitude hard to understand. The doctrine had been announced: "If we build tunnels, we shall be immune, or at least we shall be able to protect our people from the worst effects of atomic attack." They spoke about the benefits provided by the tunnels with an assurance that was not always shared by their visitors, and they were inclined to be contemptuous when we told them that civil defense against air raids has been virtually abandoned in the United States, because in our eyes the problem seems to be insoluble and the only defense lies in massive retaliation.

"So you are doing nothing—nothing at all?" we were asked.

"That is right. We do not think anything can be done that makes any sense. The government has built deep shelters near Washington for itself and the military command at the cost of millions of dollars, but most of us feel it is a waste of money. The government survives, while the people perish. We do not think this is a solution."

"But the Russians are also tunneling underground," we were told. "They have the most efficient system of civil defense in the world. This we know. It is incomprehensible to us that you do nothing. You say the government has dug shelters for itself but not for the people. That means that the ruling capitalist class protects itself and does not care for the people. In China our government cares for the people."

We assured them it was not as simple as that. There are problems that absolutely defy solution. There are problems of such magnitude that no solution can be conceived: God, death, the nature of the universe. An atomic attack followed by the annihilation of nearly all living creatures is of this order. I said: "There are many of us in the United States who are not convinced that the tunnels will save many lives. The tunnels may be a trap, like the Maginot Line. It is not a question of burying oneself deep in the earth and then coming up again a few hours or days later. It is a question of how you can live when the air is poisoned."

They took us down into the tunnels beneath Tsingtao. A long narrow flight of steps led twenty feet down into the earth into a tunnel about eight feet wide and ten feet high with a rounded ceiling. Electric lights hung overhead, throwing our shadows on the red brick floor. The walls were faced with stone and concrete. We marched in single file for about two hundred yards, and then there would be an abrupt right-angle turn and we would go on for another two hundred yards. Sometimes there were steps and we found ourselves dropping down another fifteen or twenty feet. Suddenly, after we had walked for twenty minutes, the tunnel opened out into a hospital with two operating rooms, and a little later it opened onto a restaurant that could hold about three hundred people if they sat quite close to one another. The equipment in the hospital was rather primitive, the restaurant was not in use; both rooms were faced with white tiles and scrupulously clean. The guide was telling us that the tunnels had been dug by volunteers directed by the revolutionary committees, there were therefore no labor costs, while the stone and concrete had been supplied free or at cost, with the result that this entire elaborate system of tunneling had weighed light as a feather on the economy.

"We think the only solution is a total ban on atomic bombs—anything less is useless. In an atomic war we are all doomed. There may be some remote regions of the world where some people will survive, but they will survive in a world not worth living in. And then there are the shock waves. Do you really think the tunnel will stand up against the shock waves?"

They looked at me pityingly.

"We have good engineers who have calculated everything," they said. "We are satisfied that we can get all the people off the streets of Tsingtao in five minutes and that all of them will survive."

I admired their self-confidence, but did not share it. A fashion had been established: all important cities must be honeycombed with tunnels. The idea derived probably from the Yenan days of the Chinese Communists, when everyone lived in caves carved out of the loess hills. These caves provided absolute safety from air attacks at a time when the Kuomintang could deliver only hundred-pound bombs: but no one expected the Russians to send down hundred-pound bombs. And there was perhaps another explanation dating back to the days of the Long March. Chiang Kai-shek's airplanes pursued the Communists through Szechuan, Kweichow and Yunnan, losing the trail only when the Communists were marching through the unknown borderlands of Tibet. The airplanes bombed the columns and strafed them with machine-gun bullets. Mao Tse-tung was terrified of the airplanes until he observed how little damage they did. Innumerable bombs and great quantities of ammunition were expended, and when the airplanes went away the Communists would sometimes discover that a horse had been killed or that a soldier had suffered a grazing wound. Thereafter Mao Tse-tung was contemptuous of airplanes.

Some time later, when we visited the tunnels in Peking, we heard exactly the same arguments. The entire city could be cleared in a few minutes, everyone knew the place he was expected to occupy in the tunnel, everything needful to support life underground had been provided, there was an advanced ventilation system, martial music was piped in, nothing could possibly go wrong. The Peking tunnels were more elaborate than the Tsingtao tunnels, and a little wider. There was fluorescent lighting, tiled floors, an appearance of subterranean opulence. We sat in a vast hall fifty feet under the earth beside an enormous lace-covered table, while an officer showed us on an illuminated map the full extent of the tunnel system under Peking. The map lit up like a pinball machine. An embroidered silk painting of plum blossoms hung on the walls. "We have achieved, thanks to our great leader and teacher . . . " But what exactly had been achieved except a false sense of security? Was it to be expected that the Russians did not already possess an accurate plan of the tunnel system?

For half an hour we walked through the tunnels and then found ourselves climbing some steps. Then someone pressed a button, a wooden roof slid silently away, and we came out in the lingerie department of a department store.

The Aquarium

The only warship we saw in Tsingtao was a small destroyer anchored off the large blue island across the bay, the island from which the city derives its name, for Tsingtao means "Blue Island." We saw many sailors in the streets but there were more soldiers; and if, as they said, Tsingtao was an important naval base, it was also an army base. We had thought of it as a seaside resort of no particular importance. We were wrong. It had a character of its own which owed very little to the Germans, who occupied it from 1899 until 1914, or to the Japanese, who occupied it from 1914 until 1922 and again from 1938 until 1945. The Germans left their church and huge baronial mansions on the seashore, but there was no trace of any influence left by the Japanese.

We came to like the city, for the people walked briskly, smiled easily, and seemed at ease. In Canton we thought we detected a heaviness of spirit, a sullenness in the population, as though they were living under strain, and it was the same in Hangchow and Tsinan. But in Tsingtao there was no sense of strain and for the first time there was the feeling that life was enjoyable. A government-employed antique dealer, an old man, a hunchback, with the best collection of antiques I had seen in China, told me he had left Peking twenty years ago. I asked him why he had left the place where the best antiques were to be found. "There is nowhere better than Tsingtao," he said. "The sea air is very pleasant, and the people of Shantung are not stiff-necked." In Peking the Shantungese are regarded as provincials with little taste for or understanding of the good things of life, careless and improvident, possessing neither the fire of the Hunanese nor the hot-blooded directness of the Szechuanese, neither intelligent nor well-mannered, neither astute nor businesslike. Nevertheless Shantung has produced more than its fair share of good poets, writers, and generals. "I shall never return to Peking," the antique dealer went on. "What is to be gained? I knew that the old days of the antique dealers were over. So I came here and live quietly and have no regrets, even though few visitors come here. I am very happy in my little shop."

So he was, as he bobbed up and down in his shop no more than five minutes' walk from the sea, his old face wreathed in smiles. In one corner of the room there was a bundle of old scroll paintings, and he was very patient as he unrolled them, one after another. There were three or four I would have bought if they had not been so expensive. I bought a long hanging scroll of Kuan Yin, the Goddess of Mercy, sitting at the foot of a foaming waterfall, a painting made toward the end of the Ching dynasty and marked down, I suppose, because it was a religious subject. It was a pleasant painting: in four or five quick strokes of the brush the artist had suggested the complicated folds of her gown, and with four or five more strokes he had painted the vase of flowers set down on the rocky ledge beside her. The waterfall was a raging torrent, and Kuan Yin's face was stern and majestic. She was the fountain of all blessings, her responsibility so great that she did not permit herself to smile, and in this she resembled the early Italian representations of the Virgin, which are severe, intellectual, full of power and authority. I also bought a small bronze bowl stamped underneath with the familiar seal of the Ming dynasty and possessing in spite of its small size the wonderful roundness and amplitude which characterizes all the works of this dynasty. The old antique dealer waved his hand toward the glass shelves laden with jades and many other precious objects.

"You are a rich American, and you buy so little," he said, not unkindly.

I told him I was not rich and had bought all the objects I could afford, and he lowered his voice and said: "Since when have the Americans become poor?"

When I think of Tsingtao I remember the kindliness of the people, the ghostly church, the little antique shop, and the aquarium set on a rocky crag overlooking the sea. There was a marine museum no more interesting than marine museums elsewhere, full of the bones of fish and crabs and dead sea creatures bottled in formaldehyde, and some large stuffed sharks. The aquarium was something else. At first sight everything was against it: it was not well kept, the water in many of the tanks was muddy, there was little light, the designer had not the faintest idea how to design an aquarium, and there was the smell of dead fish. It looked altogether uninviting, and I came to the conclusion that it had been designed by some German architect in the days when the main street of Tsingtao was called Bismarckstrasse. Even the fish seemed to be German. There were scaly zeppelin-like fish with fierce eyes and fat bulbous fish with snapping mouths who looked as though they would enjoy swallowing each other, and there were writhing eels gasping for air, their heads all lying close to an air vent, while their long tails danced obscenely. There were giant sea turtles said to be three hundred years old. They never moved, never opened their leathery eyelids, and could be presumed dead. There were fish that looked like sea slugs and there were starfish with strange black and silver markings. But all this was merely the prelude to the single most brilliant display of Chinese angelfish I have ever seen.

These enchanting creatures were about an inch long, in all colors from blue to reddish-gold, with long filmy fins resembling wings. There were about twenty of them, darting about in all directions, seeming to have no purpose in life except to display their bright plumage and their iridescent colors. They darted about at fantastic speed, giving themselves up to a wild joy in life. Some wings were four or five inches long, and sometimes they appeared to be rejoicing for the pure pleasure of rejoicing. When they suddenly turned corners and darted in another direction altogether, it was beyond belief that they had any reason to change direction. No: the maneuver was accomplished to allow them to display the elaborate beauty of their long shimmering wings and the intense brilliance of their coloring, for at the precise moment when they turned they seemed to shoot out sparks of light. Full of envy, I was contemplating their perfect freedom when I became aware of a portly gentleman at my side.

"You can see they are happy," he said soberly. "They must have been reading from Mao Tse-tung's little red book."

A Hospital and a Beer Factory

There came a time when each of us became aware of the constraints placed upon us. We were not free to go where we pleased; we rarely saw the Chinese in their houses; a heavy schedule had been arranged for us, and we were obliged to follow the schedule exactly. At the beginning most of us were happy to be led about. By the middle of the journey a few of us were seriously wondering whether there might not be a better way to travel through China. What bothered us most of all was the time wasted when we were taken to a factory and had to listen to an interminable speech of welcome and a long description of how the factory operated under the benevolent guidance of the revolutionary committee always fully obedient to the precepts of Mao Tse-tung and determinedly opposed to the counterrevolutionary efforts of the Gang of Four. Long hours were consumed in these pleasantries, and we were usually exhausted before we set out to inspect the factory.

Some of us thought it would be better if we divided into smaller groups. Those who were interested in factories would visit factories; those who wanted to see hospitals would visit hospitals; those who wanted to see schools would visit schools. The guides strongly objected, saying it would be too complicated, we would get lost, no provision had been made for small groups, and long practice had shown that the present method was superior to all others. My own feeling was that they had made a serious error. A law had been handed down: "All groups shall maintain a precise schedule and no one shall be allowed to stray from the group." The guides enjoyed their authority; they had not thought out the problem; and their authority stood between us and the Chinese.

At first we were scarcely aware that the problem existed, for in the early days we were spellbound by the new China. We were seeing a country of great beauty, which the Chinese Communists had made more beautiful by insisting that every acre of agricultural land be plowed and tilled. We saw China through a mist of legends. The whole country was mourning its dead leader and at the same time it was being subjected to propaganda vilifying the dead leader's widow. We remained respectful. We had come to China to learn. We learned many good things, but we were learning too that the heads of revolutionary committees were pretentious bureaucrats who rejoiced in their positions of power and authority. Their pompous speeches bored us to death: we had heard so many of them that we could recite them in our sleep. And slowly it was beginning to occur to us that these bureaucrats were perhaps not altogether beloved by the people they ruled over. We began to watch them more carefully as they led us around their factories. We observed that they had the manner of factory owners. It was their factory; they gave the orders; they were in absolute command. The workers treated them deferentially. There was no feeling of comradeship. There were the bosses earning between two hundred and three hundred yuan a month, and there were the workers earning forty yuan a month, and there was no common ground between them. Mao Tse-tung's efforts to humanize the bureaucrats had failed.

At Tsingtao, near the end of the journey, we found ourselves asking harder questions. How was the revolutionary committee chosen? We had assumed it was elected by the whole body of the workers, and learned that it was appointed by the local authorities. Why were women paid less than men? There were whispered consultations, and then the chairman of the revolutionary committee announced that it was not so, women were absolutely equal to men, and if, as sometimes happened, there was a difference in their wages, then that could be explained by the different tasks they were asked to perform. We would ask him what his own salary was, and he would reply that the average wage in the factory was sixty yuan. Yes, but your salary? He smiled, waved his hand, turned to answer another question, and made a speech about the freedom enjoyed by everyone in China as compared with the virtual slavery under the feudal regime of the past when no one, absolutely no one, was his own master. The speech was a long one. We had heard exactly the same speech the previous day.

We went to a hospital on a bluff overlooking the sea. It was large, spacious, comfortable. The soft sea-winds came through the open windows. Once more there was tranquillity, a quiet purposefulness. The doctors were experimenting with new techniques involving diathermal machines, deep-sleep therapy, electric vibrators. In room after room patients were lying prostrate on their beds, expressionless and unconscious, with instruments attached to their arms, heads, and legs. At first it was frightening, for they looked like corpses. It was less frightening when you approached closer to them: it was almost possible to see the health pouring into them from the machines. One of the doctors laughed: "The sea air cures them. We just pretend to cure them." Behind the hospital, on a hill, stood a pagoda that must date from the Sung dynasty. It was nobly proportioned and threw a protective shadow over the hospital.

We went to see an embroidery factory, a cloth-dyeing factory, and a beer factory. I do not think we learned very much from them except that factory work is brutally repetitive and mechanical. Fifteen- or sixteen-year-old girls were busy at the long tables working over their embroidery. The designs were traditional: flowers, peacocks, kittens. None of the designs had any life in them. Sometimes with the aid of a mechanical duplicator the girls were able to embroider two or more pieces of cloth simultaneously They looked pale; they were all hurrying to finish their quotas in time, silent, intent upon their work, like robots. There was no joy in it. For their labors they received thirty-six yuan a month, about twenty dollars.

Embroidery is still very largely a human occupation, depending on a constant supply of nimble-fingered girls. Cloth-dyeing is mechanical. In a vast workshop with twenty machines there would be no more than a dozen workmen. Endless bolts of cloth ten feet wide poured out of the vats and were smoothed and dried out and finally neatly folded after being drawn through rolling machines covering a space as large as a football field. The thundering roar of the machines drowned all conversation. The workmen did not look happy, but probably there are no happy workmen in cloth-dyeing factories anywhere in the world.

At the Tsingtao beer factory we were permitted to drink unlimited amounts of beer, and became tipsy. The convivial chairman of the revolutionary committee drank to the memory of Chairman Mao Tse-tung and to the health of Chairman Hua Kuo-feng, and for each toast we drank about a gallon of beer. Glasses were miraculously filled by waiters who smiled at us approvingly, ingratiatingly. Why a beer factory in Tsingtao? This was easy to explain. The Germans had founded it in 1903, and it had continued except for occasional interruptions due to war and mischance for nearly three quarters of a century. We asked what exactly was meant by "mischance," and were told that there had been some occasions when the imperialist powers had deliberately held up the operations of the beer factory by refusing to allow the export of hops. The imperialist powers did not want the Chinese to drink beer. Why? This was not explained. But the "mischance" would never happen again, because hop seeds had been smuggled

Buddha in Four Gate Temple, near Tsinan.

Buddha on Thousand Buddha Cliffs, near Tsinan.

Pagoda near Tsinan.

Four Gate Temple near Tsinan.

German cathedral at Tsingtao.

Official art in Tsingtao brewery.

Temple of Yo Fei, Hangchow.

The Yellow River near Tsinan.

out of Europe and hops were now growing healthily only a few miles from the factory. Charts were held up for our inspection, and we learned that the Tsingtao beer factory manufactured 300 tons of beer in 1923, 1,200 tons in 1949, when the Chinese Communists came to power, 11,400 tons in 1965, and 30,000 tons in 1975. "Thus you see that under the benevolent guidance of Chairman Mao Tse-tung we have increased the production of beer twenty-four times since liberation."

We applauded the prodigious increase in production, while the chairman of the revolutionary committee, who appeared to have a limitless capacity for beer, beamed at us, saying that the factory workers were enthusiastically calling for the destruction of the Gang of Four. We were reminded that Chairman Mao Tse-tung had advanced the cause of beer drinking by being a good beer drinker. As a result of the efforts of the workers and the Chinese Communist party, Tsingtao beer was being sold all over the world, even in the United States. He hoped that very shortly the production figure would reach 50,000 tons. The beer tasted like Karlsberg beer and was very strong.

We staggered out into the dying sunlight, and that night we took the train for Peking, drunk and jubilant.

NOTES FROM A DIARY

When I was in China during the war, in every street I used to see dead and rotting rats with blood and pus pouring out of them. There were no garbage collectors and the rats lay there for days until they disintegrated or were carried away by the rains. In the poor neighborhoods every tenth child suffered from glaucoma and every second child was undernourished. In Chungking a quarter of a million people lived in mat-shed huts, clinging to the huge rock that jutted over the Yangtse and the Chialing rivers. The Chungking summers were equatorial, and the winters were dark under a heavy gray cloud that formed at the confluence of the two rivers, blocking out the sun for four months every year. The cloud saved us from Japanese air attacks, but it bred disease among the people of Chungking, killed them off in their hundreds of thousands, sucked away the vitality of the survivors, and their will to live. A doctor said: "We need more dispensaries for the poor, vitamins, sulfa drugs, more X-ray machines, home care for nursing mothers—we need so many things that we cannot even begin to make a list of them. When we ask for these things, we are told that military equipment must have priority, but the Nationalist army isn't fighting. All the military equipment is being hoarded for the coming war against the Chinese Communists. Well, it will do no good to them. The Nationalists may be able to sweep the Chinese Communists off the face of the earth, but that will not solve the problem. The problem is a simple one: the poor have nowhere to turn to. Sooner or later—and much sooner than you think—the poor will blow this stupid government to smithereens. What this government lacks is responsibility to the people. They don't care!"

That was in Chungking in the summer of 1942. Four years later I was in Yenan. Chu Teh, the commander in chief of the Red Army, was talking about the cave hospital cut out of the loess hills a few hundred yards from his headquarters. It was not a large hospital, for there were only about thirty beds. Chu Teh was sixty, but looked much older. He resembled an old, gnarled peasant, kindly and humorous, with a glint of steel in his eyes. He had no mannerisms and dressed as simply as his soldiers. He said: "We need medical supplies so much—for the people and for the soldiers. You have seen the hospital. There is almost nothing there—almost no drugs, no medicines, no chloroform. We wash and rewash old bandages until they fall to pieces in our hands. Since you are going to London, I want you to ask the British government to send us medical supplies. There is no difficulty in bringing them to us, because we have just captured the port of Chefoo. If they will send us medical supplies, we will be eternally grateful."

As he talked about medical supplies, he looked careworn, his face deeply weathered, his wide mouth set in a firm line.

"You understand, we don't need weapons, because we can always capture them from the enemy. But medical supplies—this is something else. We need them terribly for our people."

I said something about the port of Chefoo being blockaded by Nationalist warships.

"It doesn't matter. We can always break the blockade. You'll see. Send us a ship with medical supplies and I promise you we will break the blockade."

In the following month I was in London and went to see the permanent secretary of the Foreign Office.

"What you are asking us to do is to tear up diplomatic rules. We have an ambassador with Chiang Kai-shek; we don't have an ambassador with Chu Teh and Mao Tse-tung. We do not acknowledge their existence. I am afraid I cannot accede to your request."

I said: "They are going to win."

"That is your opinion. It is no more than an opinion. Tell me, what will he win with? Guns? He hasn't any. Airplanes? He hasn't any. Tanks? He hasn't any. What has he got?"

"Soldiers, about two million of them under arms."

He looked surprised.

"Those are not *our* figures."

"No, they are his figures."

"And you believe them?"

"Of course."

He paused for a moment and looked through the window at St. James's Park misty on a September afternoon.

He said: "How many soldiers did you see?"

"One. He was a courier racing across the valley toward Chu Teh's headquarters!"

"One soldier!" he exclaimed. "By God, you saw one soldier! One soldier! What a joke! The Chinese Communist army—two million men—and you saw one soldier! By this time next year I assure you we will be hearing a good deal less about the Chinese Communists!"

Chu Teh died at the age of ninety-two a few months ago. I remember the dead rats of Chungking and how nobody cared what happened to the poor and the sick under the regime of Chiang Kai-shek, and I think of Chu Teh in his cave, the deep lines on his face and his look of misery when he spoke about washing and rewashing the bandages until they fell to pieces in the nurses' hands, and it seems to me that it will always be like this: those who care will win, and those who do not care will go down to everlasting hell.

We were talking about Buddhism with our guides. It appears that during the Great Proletarian Cultural Revolution Buddhism was officially proscribed. The Red Guards were let loose on Buddhist temples and anyone in a monk's gown was in danger of being thrown into prison, or worse. A few former Buddhist monks were employed as curators of important temples, but this was the extent of their employment. What happened to the rest of them?

"They work in the factories or the communes," the guide said. "They have been reeducated."

"Are there no priests celebrating religious services anywhere in China?"

"No, it is forbidden. Religion is the opium of the people. As you know, we have given up opium too."

"What about the museums?"

He stared hard, trying to think what possible connection there was between a Buddhist monk and a museum.

"It so happens that about a third of the surviving pieces of Chinese art are directly or indirectly connected with Buddhism. If you destroy the Buddhist priesthood, you make it much more difficult to understand Buddhist art. You are destroying part of your heritage."

"No."

"What does no mean?"

"Buddhism is part of our feudal past. It was used to make us bow down to our temporal and spiritual lords. It was a yoke round our necks. Thanks to our great teacher and leader Chairman Mao Tse-tung we have learned that Buddhism was a feudal and capitalist instrument for oppressing the poor. Do you know what the Buddhist lamas were doing in Tibet? When they built a new lamasery they sacrificed babies and buried them at the four corners of the temples. And not only babies but also grown men, grown women, and children! So much for this Buddhist culture you seem to regard so highly! We have seen films of Tibet before liberation, terrible films! The lamas have been swept away and now the Tibetans live under socialism, and they study Marx, Engels, Lenin, Stalin, and Mao Tse-tung instead of the meaningless sutras they studied previously."

"And you—do you study all these?"

"No, I only study Mao Tse-tung. For centuries the Chinese will be studying Mao Tse-tung! We believe in him firmly! I would go anywhere he wanted me to go and do whatever he wanted me to do—"

"But he is dead?"

"No, he is alive in our hearts!"

I have no doubt he was telling the truth as he saw it. In his mind Mao Tse-tung was the Moses who was given the inexpressible privilege of handing down the tablets of the law; but after Moses came other prophets and after the chosen people reached the promised land they entered the fires of exile. In an extraordinary way the history of China during the last thirty years has been the history of Mao Tse-tung. He dominated the masses to the ultimate degree. As he grew older and less sure of himself, he continued to dominate them because the machinery of domination was already established. Time stood still, while the man who sometimes called himself "the old monk walking the world with a leaky umbrella" looked down at his handiwork with mingled happiness and despair.

We have been to three or four kindergartens and two primary schools. The children are always clean, well dressed, and obviously well fed. The teachers look somewhat nervous, and I suspect that they are not well paid and the chairman of the revolutionary committee leans hard on them. For some reason, when we enter a classroom the children are invariably being taught to say in English or Chinese: "Down with the Gang of Four." Sometimes they add the names of the conspirators, Chiang Ching, Chang Chun-chiao, Wang Hung-wen, and Yao Wen-yuan, names which we can now recite in our sleep.

When a teacher points to a child and asks a question, the child immediately rises, snaps to attention, answers the question clearly, sits down, and abruptly folds his arms. At such times he looks like an automaton. But when we leave the classroom the children are all smiles, clapping merrily.

The government is evidently determined that five-year-olds should hate the Gang of Four. In the garden of a kindergarten we found a round target with the face of Chiang Ching painted on it. If you hit it with a stone, the target revolved on a spindle to reveal the scowling face of Chang Chun-chiao, the hated former mayor of Shanghai who until recently was the senior deputy prime minister and chief political officer of the armed forces.

I have been thinking of André Malraux and wondering what he would make of the new China which he last visited in 1965, although he spent a good deal of his life living in an imaginary China. He had more in common with Mao

Tse-tung than anyone I know. The poetry, the daring, the sense of being dedicated to extraordinary achievements, the refusal to believe that there are any limitations to the power of the human spirit, all this he shared with Mao Tse-tung. I believe that if ever he had achieved real power, he would have acted like Mao Tse-tung—he would have resolved problems by tearing them up by the roots. Twice he achieved some political power: once when he equipped the Spanish Republican air force and sent it out against Franco's immensely more powerful forces, and then again when he became General de Gaulle's chief adviser during the time when France was cutting off its ties with Algeria. The first involved astonishing courage (the Long March), the second involved "removing the jawbone because a tooth is infected" (Mao's actions when in power). There was a third quality they had in common: the *farfelu*, the sense of fantasy, of that many-colored thread of nonsense that runs through the universe. We see it sometimes in Mao's poems and in his calligraphy and in his description of himself as the Foolish Old Man of the Mountain. There was an anarchic fire in both of them, and at the same time they were highly disciplined men. Anarchy and order form a dazzling combination—and move mountains.

I say "I have been thinking of André Malraux" as though this was something unusual. In fact I think of him daily, hourly; he is the best of imaginary companions, because he talked brilliantly about every subject under the sun. This afternoon it occurred to me that though I have lunched with him at Lasserre and talked with him in his white and gold ministerial office in the Palais Royale, I have never seen him in the open air. In particular I have never wandered with him through China and never visited with him a Buddhist site with the sculptures still in place—those sculptures that he loved almost to distraction. I would have given a great deal to have been with him when we visited the Buddhist monastery and the Four Gate Temple. I imagine him examining that small and perfect temple for five minutes and then discoursing upon it for a whole hour with a wild and raging eloquence, scarcely taking breath. Now when I think of Malraux I shall imagine him sitting under the walnut trees in sight of that temple, leaning forward, his sharp nose cutting the air, his enormous eyes feasting on a building smaller than any cottage, one of the loveliest things in all of China.

It occurs to me that historians will have great difficulty recording the last years of the life of Mao Tse-tung. He lived in seclusion in his well-guarded villa near the North Lake in Peking and in another villa in the Western Hills; he read, studied, handed down pronouncements, received occasional visitors, and lived apart from the world. For most of his life, except during the Long March, he was in remarkably good health, but during the last ten years he suffered from heart disease and was forbidden by his doctors to do anything that would excite him. He was given restoratives from the Chinese pharmacopoeia. They prolonged his life but exhausted him, and he began to age rapidly. From about 1968 onward his health was definitely failing. He made no speeches, handed down very few directives, met very few people, and became more and more a recluse, leaving the burden of government to Chou En-lai, who was also ailing. In consequence the government of China faltered.

From the very beginning of his revolutionary career Mao Tse-tung was bitterly critical of bureaucrats, especially of revolutionary bureaucrats. They possessed, he believed, a particular attitude of mind which was endlessly self-serving and endlessly deadening. In the years of his decline the bureaucrats took charge, while Chiang Ching proclaimed herself to be the standard-bearer of the radicals who at least preserved the purity of the revolutionary flame. The bureaucrats left her alone, for they had their own fields to plow, and in spite of her control of newspapers, films and the theater, she was rarely able to impose her will on them. She had carved out her small empire; they, too, had carved out their small empires. And both in their differing ways were self-serving and deadening. For all their talk of "revolutionary committees" and "revolutionary action," they were stifling the revolution. They created huge, unwieldy machines which continued to exist only because they had acquired momentum and because they proclaimed that they spoke in the name of Mao Tse-tung.

In Chinese history the emperor was always secluded, and in theory he was all the more powerful the more he held himself at a remote distance from the people. In fact, Mao Tse-tung's real power was withering away and he appears to have been aware of it, to have resented it, and to have made various attempts to regain it but without success, chiefly because he was too old to fight and because there were people close to him who had no desire to change the status quo. Chou En-lai's energies were being dissipated in the countless day-by-day operations of the government. Nor was he, in spite of his brilliance, a man capable of sweeping away the accumulated rubbish of a revolution that seemed to have got out of hand, uncontrollably at the mercy of the bureaucrats and a small but vociferous band of people who called themselves radicals and were out for mischief. The Gang of Four is now described as reactionary, they are accused of having taken the capitalist road and of having used the public till for their own pleasures. They were adventurists out of touch with the people. What is puzzling is that they could have endured for so long and that Chou En-lai was unable to stop them. The explanation appears to be that they had built up their own enclave in Shanghai and were out of his reach, and that they were or seemed to be under the protection of Mao Tse-tung.

PEKING

The Visionary City

From the sixteenth floor of the Peking Hotel I looked out in the early morning light at the city shrouded in mist and slowly coming to life. Very faintly there could be discerned the shapes of the Forbidden City, but there was no color in it, only the swirling mist under the frozen skies. And then gradually the mist began to dissolve and break away, and the yellow roofs of the palaces began to emerge far below like yellow fishes at the bottom of a murky pool. They seemed to be without substance, floating there, saucer-shaped, curling at the edges, almost transparent, without any texture, moving slowly—a whole shoal of yellow fishes. And then the mist swept over them again and hid them.

The Peking Hotel beneficently provides a small balcony for each of the rooms overlooking the Forbidden City. I sat on the balcony in the cold wind, studying the mist: a peculiarly Chinese occupation. The wind was beating against the upper stories of the hotel, but apparently was showing not the slightest interest in the vast city lying below, still drowning in mist. Suddenly, for no apparent reason, the mist began to boil like milk and then mysteriously vanished, leaving only a few shreds clinging to the northern part of the city. The yellow roofs were gleaming with the moisture left by the mist, almost silvery. Soon the moisture drained away and the entire imperial city was flashing in the winter sunlight. What appeared to be a hundred golden palaces lay below in immaculate order, like jewels carefully arranged at the bottom of a jewel box. From the sixteenth floor of the hotel even the largest palaces looked as though they had been made for dwarfs.

I had known Peking in late spring and summer, but never in winter. For some reason I often dreamed about it in winter, the snow falling, the camels from Mongolia wandering through the icy streets, the lakes frozen over, and icicles hanging from the roofs of the palaces. It seemed to me that Peking in summer was magnificence enough, even when the dust storms blew in from the Gobi Desert or sudden rainstorms cleared the wide streets, but in winter it would be the purest perfection, all gold and yellow and white. And so it was, but not in the way I had expected.

I went down to the hotel lobby, which was more than forty feet high, with enormous gilded columns exactly like the columns that appear in the throne rooms of the emperors in the Forbidden City. Against a red background in gold letters were the words: *We have friends in every country in the world,* and there was about this inscription, set near the banks of elevators, what appeared to be a note of defiance and also of enduring hope, as though the Communist regime was announcing with great deliberation that its influence spread out over all the lands below heaven and that it was no longer a hermit kingdom. For the word *world* in the inscription they use the phrase *tien hsia,* which means "under heaven" and by extension "everything that is under heaven." The imperial magnificence of the inscription should not blind us to the fact that it is not quite true. The Chinese, for example, appear to have very few friends in the Soviet Union.

Today when stories about the misdeeds of the Gang of Four are legion, and many of them are true, it does no harm to tell one more. The story goes that Chou En-lai, who possessed excellent taste, gave orders to the architects to design the new Peking Hotel in such a way (1) that it would not totally overwhelm the old one, which was to remain virtually untouched, and (2) that it should not be festooned with political propaganda pictures; instead the paintings on the walls should be views of China, not those views which show Red Army soldiers in the foreground with towering mountains in the background, but quite simply the most beautiful views without any Red Army soldiers at all. Chiang Ching heard about this and led a deputation of protesters. She insisted that in the main dining hall of the Peking Hotel there should be a vast and monumental portrait of Mao Tse-tung either at the moment when he declared the birth of the People's Republic of China or at some period during the Long March, where he would be seen standing in a commanding position with a red flag behind him. Chou En-lai argued with her very patiently. He pointed out that he was responsible for funding the hotel, which cost untold millions of yuan, and that it had been agreed by the Central Committee that he should be completely in charge. Chiang Ching replied that she was wholly responsible for the arts of China and therefore must be consulted on everything concerned with the design of the hotel and especially with the paintings. She stamped her feet, she insisted, she pleaded. Chou En-lai went to Mao Tse-tung and explained the situation. He said he entirely approved of a statue of Chairman Mao

Tse-tung in the dining room, but the huge painting on the wall would have the effect of overawing the visitors and distinguished guests; and there was another point that should not be taken lightly: since all or nearly all the tables were circular, there would be guests sitting with their backs turned to the portrait. He concluded that it would be much better to have a spectacular painting of some scenery in China and he proposed that the artist should be allowed to choose his own subject. Mao Tse-tung was convinced by these arguments, and so it came about that the great dining hall of the Peking Hotel has a breathtaking painting of the towering volcanic mountains of Kweilin with a river flowing below. The mountains are green with summer, the river is the blue of a child's paint box, and the pleasure boats on the river are all the colors of the rainbow. The painting, which is one hundred feet long and sixty feet high, is by no means a masterpiece, but it is pleasant, restful, and monumental. It is as though the whole wall had been transformed into a window on Kweilin.

The dining room was an act of the imagination with implications going far beyond the normal preoccupations of politicians. There were lessons to be learned from it, particularly the lesson that sometimes the best propaganda is no propaganda and that a surfeit of propaganda is a weariness of the flesh and a misery on the eyes. Here propaganda came to a halt, and there was not even one of those ghostly white statues of Mao Tse-tung made of gypsum that have been put up wherever there is a gap in the scenery. While we ate our eight-course meals we feasted on the beauty of Kweilin.

The new Peking Hotel and the old Peking Hotel live in harmony. One is vast, functional, silent, gleaming like well-oiled machinery; the other is dark, noisy with creaking stairs, inhabited by many ghosts. A passageway leads from one to the other; it is a passageway between two worlds. Here, or perhaps over there, was Henri Veitch's bookshop, where generations of Peking University students acquired a taste for French literature. His books were expensive, his manners were impeccable, he had read every French book worth reading, and he was himself a university. He also published books and enjoyed giving extempore lectures on all subjects under the sun. He was part of the Peking that has gone forever.

Gone forever? We are always being told that the old Peking has gone forever. But my first outing in the city suggested that the old Peking of thirty years ago or five hundred years ago was still there. What had changed were the costumes, for everyone wore drab clothes, padded coats, padded trousers, in dark modulations of blue, gray and black, and the shapeless workingmen's caps were not designed to frame a face. The caps are ugly, lumpy, and may have been made of sailcloth left out in the rain. The shops have not changed overmuch except that there are more of them. The shopkeepers are polite, interested, ceremonial; their faces are kindly, and they will go to no end of trouble to find what you want, with smiles and a gentle sweeping of the arms. The shops are crowded and there are huge covered marketplaces where you can buy anything from pharmaceuticals to rare books. With an elderly gentleman of the old school I went to a food shop. Prices are marked on a blackboard above the cashier's desk; first you pay for what you are going to eat, and then you sit down at one of the rickety tables and wait for the waitress to bring your order—tea, noodles, and sweet doughnuts. This is new. On the sidewalks the peasants from the surrounding communes pile mountains of fresh vegetables and sell them to anyone who wants them, thus sidetracking the official marketplaces. This, too, is new. It was unthinkable in the old days that anyone would be allowed to pile mountains of anything in the streets, just as it was unthinkable that you would pay for food before you ate it. The price of a meal for two now came to about fifty cents; it would have been a little more expensive in the old days.

In Peking people walk more slowly than in Shanghai. There is an air of leisure. Even when the snow began to fall late in the morning they did not hurry their pace, and nearly everyone had a companion. In Shanghai half the people seemed to be walking alone and in Peking only about one-tenth of the people walk alone. Life in Peking is for talking, telling stories, companionship. I ask: "Where are the camels?" and my elderly friend tells me a long story about the life of a camel driver he knew in the days when camels came in droves to Peking from the Mongolian plains, but never answers the question. Where are they? Have they vanished? Is their disappearance one more of the vagaries inflicted on Peking by the Great Proletarian Cultural Revolution? Or have they gone like the rickshaw and the old Manchu mandarins in their long robes of silk or sable?

"You understand, we are all proletarians here," the old man said, and I would have believed him more readily if I had not heard the same words from Lao Wu.

Outwardly, yes. Of course they are more proletarian, and just as obviously there are comparatively few faces in Peking which have the authentic proletarian look. I observe that even Mao jackets can be cut in such a way that they no longer look like a uniform. Mao Tse-tung said long ago that the people of Peking were stubborn in their ways and needed to be constantly reminded that a revolution had taken place. They regarded themselves as a people apart as distinguished from the Hunanese, who regarded themselves as people of the heartland, close to the earth. Perhaps; but it was Peking that transformed him into an emperor. I asked my companion what he really thought of Mao Tse-tung. He said: "There was Robespierre and then came Napoleon, which was worse. There was Lenin and then came Stalin, which was worse, and this is what revolution is all about."

"So you expect the worst?"

"No, I belong to Peking. We always expect the better."

On that day the snow came down steadily, turning to slush in the streets. But on the high curved roofs the snow remained and if you looked up you saw a visionary city, white and glowing under a dull sky, with immense gate towers and palaces, all turning to ice, and it looked like Coleridge's city:

> In Xanadu did Kubla Khan
>   A stately pleasure-dome decree:
> Where Alph, the sacred river, ran
> Through caverns measureless to man
>   Down to a sunless sea. . . .
>
> That sunny dome! those caves of ice!
> And all who heard should see them there,
> And all should cry, Beware! Beware!
> His flashing eyes, his floating hair!
> Weave a circle round him thrice,
> And close your eyes with holy dread,
> For he on honey-dew hath fed,
> And drunk the milk of Paradise.

The Great Wall of China

They used to say of the Great Wall of China that it was the only man-made thing in the world that could be seen with the naked eye from the moon, but that was before any naked eyes ever appeared on the moon. My own naked eyes once regarded it fearfully from the cockpit of a DC-3 with an American pilot who amused himself by chasing it across the mountains north of Peking and then when he found a particularly high peak he would aim the airplane at it, believing that the updraft would carry us over it. He happened to be right, but it was beyond belief that he would always be right. When I think of the Great Wall, I see it coming toward me at atrocious speed, looking more like a fortress than a wall, white and gleaming in the summer sunlight, and I can distinguish every brick and shaped rock, and suddenly the invisible horns of an invisible bull rise from somewhere beneath the airplane and buck us over the edge of the mountain with only four or five feet to spare. The pilot thought this was the best of all games, and I thought it was the silliest.

Now, so many years later, I am beginning to see that the pilot was right, for it is only from an airplane that the Great Wall displays its full majesty. Now that I have seen it from the ground I have learned its limitations. Standing on it, you see it coming down one hill and going up another. No excitement; no sense of its fantastic length, its phantasmagorical clinging to the highest ridges of the highest mountains. From the air you can see thirty or forty miles of the Wall wandering merrily into the distance with an urgent life in it. It is not blocks of stone; it is color, outline, a flowing river. It does not look man-made; it looks like decoration. Above all, it never looks like a wall, is not massive, is not pretentious. It gives shape and form to the mountains and cavorts in the most gentle fashion for hundreds of mountainous miles like a river which has found its bed not in the valleys but on the highest peaks.

Today, if the Chinese government permits you to enter China, there is nothing easier than to stand on the Great

Wall. The bus, the inevitable Toyota, waits outside the Peking Hotel and takes you to it in three or four hours along broad avenues and winding mountain roads. There is the feeling of speeding northward into unknown and unmapped territory, into a kind of fairyland dominated by that mysterious Wall, which is uninhabited and now purposeless, a vestige of a long distant and terrifying past. For centuries the Chinese manned the Wall in the hope of keeping out the barbarians from the north, and for centuries the barbarians continued to climb over it. It was a monument to futility.

The guides have been telling us about its length, width and height, the various epochs in which it was built, the size of the stones, the number of guard posts, the number of times the individual stones would encircle the earth if they were laid end to end. They recite the figures tonelessly; they have learned them by heart long ago in the mistaken belief that foreigners are in love with statistics. We are not in love with statistics but in a curious, helpless way we are in love with the Wall. This puzzles the Chinese, who wonder why we have so adamantly demanded to see it. The Wall represents the ancient feudal China, which they despise more deeply than they despise anything else. One of the guides has given us a long recitation on the number of people who died in the construction of the wall and the sufferings it engendered. "This feudal age was ended by our great leader and teacher Mao Tse-tung, who put an end to the exploitation of the people by tyrannical feudal lords."

We are told that the Wall as we now see it began at the time of the Warring States many centuries before Christ and was completed during the Ming dynasty. This is not quite true. The Wall here at the Nankow Pass has obviously been refaced quite recently. Whole sections of the Wall have been restored during the last twenty years. It gleams with newness and freshness, not a single stone out of place. The Chinese Communists have also had a hand in building the Wall, but without any love for it.

This section of the Wall at the Nankow Pass is the only part of it that foreigners are allowed to see. The pass is really an abrupt canyon which has been the pathway of many invaders. The Wall curves steeply into a landscape of jagged mountains which eventually form the southeastern rim of Inner Mongolia. As the Wall climbs down to the bottom of the canyon, it is so steep that on a windy day it is almost impossible for anyone to walk along it. It is precisely this plunge into the canyon that makes the Nankow Pass so dramatic.

On this particular day a bitterly cold wind was blowing strongly. We were wrapped up in heavy blue coats lined with camel's hair, those comfortable and rugged coats which are worn everywhere in north China, and in addition most of us had fur caps with earflaps and wore gloves. Yet even now I can still feel the savagery of that cold and penetrating wind which seemed to have the power to paralyze all movement and to destroy all willpower. I became an icicle, with frozen face and freezing fingers, which had to be trained anew to use a 16 mm. movie camera. This icicle was attempting with only rudimentary success to climb a wall which stood at an angle of 45°. I was moving step by step, painfully and slowly, wondering whether I would ever reach a stone archway that incomprehensibly stood a hundred feet away from me. At this moment some red-cheeked Red Army soldiers came running up the steep slope in padded slippers, each of them breathing out white fumes of frost. They did not run very fast, but at least they were running, while I was crawling. When they reached me, they stopped running to look at the little black movie camera. I took shots of the Wall winding up the opposite side of the canyon. They listened attentively to the whirring of the machinery, nodded their heads, asked whether I was a foreigner, a question that puzzled me because I would have thought it was obvious, and then having examined the camera carefully, turning it over in their hands, they raced up the wall till they reached the curious archway, where they waved frantically. They were young and good-humored, and I have never seen redder cheeks. I observed that they stayed awhile under the archway, getting their breaths back.

Down below, at the bottom of the canyon, new busloads of visitors were entering the parking lot and unloading. There were also a surprising number of jeeps filled with Chinese army men. I wondered what official business could bring them to the Great Wall and concluded that they were all having an outing, and the Wall fascinated them as much as it fascinated us. There was the sheer majesty and magnificence of it at close hand and the delicacy of it as it wandered into the distance. It was curious how the Wall gave lightness to those mountains, which were dark and powerful, among the heaviest shapes I have ever known. This comes about, I believe, because the wall is predominately white and resembles a long fin or a thin sail and seems to be lifting the mountains up.

At last, coming down the mountain, I found a shop serving noodles and warmed myself beside an old-fashioned iron stove, grateful to be indoors, while the wind howled outside.

The same bus that took us to the Great Wall took us to the Ming tombs, or rather to the tomb of the Ming emperor Wan Li and his two empresses. He reigned from 1572 to 1619, and was therefore a contemporary of Shakespeare. He is remembered chiefly because some of the best

Ming pottery was made during his reign, which was one of the longest in Chinese history. It is recorded of him that "he loved his eunuchs too much," ruled despotically, became so fat that he could scarcely move, and enjoyed playing with the two clocks and the clavichord that the Jesuit priest Matteo Ricci presented to him. Ricci was the first European ever to enter the Forbidden City in Peking, and among the gifts he offered to the uncomprehending emperor was a fragment of the True Cross. Ricci was an intellectual of the first rank and Wan Li was quite possibly the stupidest and most extravagant of Chinese emperors. He started building his tomb when he was quite young, at a cost of eight million ounces of silver, and was so pleased with it that he held a party in the huge underground cavern where many years later he was buried.

In 1956 Chinese archeologists set about opening the tomb, which lay under a huge artificial mound thickly covered with pine trees. The difficulty was to find the secret entrance. After a few days, while they were digging, they came upon a tablet reading "This tablet is 160 feet from the sealing wall of the funeral chamber at a depth of thirty-five feet." The archeologists were a little surprised by their good fortune. A few days later, following the instructions on the tablet, they broke through a wall and found themselves looking down at an empty stone chamber with a white marble door that clearly led to another chamber. With some difficulty this door was opened, and they found another chamber, much longer, but also empty. Then came a third chamber over a hundred feet long which contained some blue and white Ming pottery and three white marble thrones: one for the emperor, decorated with dragons and clouds, and two for his empresses, carved with phoenixes. Finally, at the end of the long avenue of chambers, there came the funeral chamber with the three enormous red-lacquered coffins and a vast treasure of precious objects spilling out over the floor—porcelains, embroidered silks, jeweled crowns, jade pendants, all the luxuries of the court. The coffins were opened. Wan Li wore his dragon robes and a delicate crown of gold mesh with two golden dragons chasing the fiery pearl of immortality.

Some of these treasures, including the emperor's crown, are shown in a small museum nearby. In the funeral chamber itself huge red packing cases take the place of the lacquered coffins, and you have the feeling that you are in some subterranean railroad station and soon the train will arrive to take the boxes to their proper destination.

The Yellow Roofs

We came to the Forbidden City on one of those rare winter days when the air has a spring freshness and the sky is a deep unfaltering blue. There was no wind and you could feel the heat of the sun beating up from the earth. On such days in spring buds burst open and become flowers, birds sing madly, children scamper, and old men prepare themselves for the summer heat and the dust from the Gobi Desert thickening the air. On the following day the snow came down in earnest and Peking went into mourning.

So on this last day of spring, on December 4, the yellow roofs of the Forbidden City showed themselves in their utmost magnificence. The day seemed to be created for them, for they were etched sharply against the sky, looking so new that they might have been made yesterday. I knew the Forbidden City well and once thought I knew every stone and every pillar, every gnarled tree and hidden corner. But I had never seen it in this calm light. These yellow-roofed palaces are among the world's supreme inventions, and to see them in their perfection is to realize that architecture is the art above all arts.

No one knows who designed them, but we know that the emperor Yung Lo ordered them built in A.D. 1405 and must have approved the design and may have been responsible for the idea of having three enormous palaces one behind another in a direct line separated by vast courtyards; and as you go from one palace to another, each subtly different, you are aware that the proportions of each palace and courtyard have been calculated to the last degree of accuracy. The great double roofs with the flaring eaves dominate each courtyard. They are more than roofs: they are banners, thrones, blazing fires, golden walls, stairways, towers. There is no straight line anywhere, not even in the ridgeline, which appears to have been made with a ruler. The first of these palaces, the Hall of Supreme Harmony, is a work of supreme harmony, of calm and serenity. Gazing at it, you come to know that harmony, calm, and serenity are possible in the world because they are all present before your eyes.

Where did these roofs come from? Some say they developed out of the shapes of ancient tents, but we have no evidence that the Chinese were ever tent dwellers. They must have developed out of tile-roofed or thatch-roofed houses. Indeed, if you half close your eyes, you will see that the Hall of Supreme Harmony, which may be the most perfect single building in the world, is a long, double-roofed barn with straw thatch colored by the setting sun.

I had not seen these palaces for thirty years but it seemed to me that nothing or very little had changed. I remembered grass growing among the stones of the courtyard; there is no grass now. The Chinese Communists have taken great care of the palaces and spent vast amounts of money restoring them. The brilliantly colored wooden underpinnings of the eaves have been recently painted. I had a feeling that they had been painted a little too brightly, that the greens and reds were not quite the same as those I remembered, and that a certain shade of apple green was notably absent. Then, too, it seemed to me that the vast courtyard, which was six hundred feet long, had been even longer thirty years ago. Reluctantly I concluded that memory is unable to retain exact images of immense palaces and immense courtyards.

The best, of course, was the yellow roof, which is not so much yellow as an imperious orange color; not chrome yellow, not the color of ripened oranges, but closely related to it. This particular color rarely appears in nature. The tiles are tubular, like bamboo, and, being placed so close together, they reflect one another, and the extraordinarily rich effect produced by the rippling surface of the roof is partly due to the play of reflected light from one tile to the other. If the roof was simply a curved sheet of gold, it would not be so lustrous.

So, if you stand on the topmost step leading down to the vast courtyard, you see perfection constantly changing, for the play of light on the roof is a living thing. Everything conspires to prevent you from looking at anything else. At the foot of the Hall of Supreme Harmony there is a protective barrier of gleaming white marble balustrades, like rows of white lace, fretted and curved into strange sinuous shapes, and this rather frivolous decoration serves to counterpoint the dignity of the yellow-roofed palace, and indeed without these balustrades the palace walls would appear to rise too abruptly from the earth. The balustrades frame the lower part of the palace; they soften the outline; they are white wave caps breaking on a yellow shore.

And so as you go from one courtyard to another, you have the impression that there must be a multiplicity of palaces, each one a mirror image of the other, whereas in fact there are only three palaces subtly different from one another, and beyond the last of them are the private quarters of the emperor, small yellow-tiled buildings looking out over courtyards with gnarled trees and bronze statues of lions and cranes with here and there a memorial pillar or a carved wellhead. Here formality gives place to studied informality, and as you wander from one small courtyard to another, protected by countless walls from all the noises of the city, there is once again the illusion that these courtyards are mirror images that go on to infinity, that there is no end to this paradise of small gardens, and that one could remain here very pleasantly for the rest of one's life. Time stands still. That gnarled tree has not changed very much in the last hundred years. Here at last the emperors achieved the illusion that they were permanent.

A Simple Thing, an Exchange of Books

We met in the Foreign Languages Press, which is a vast compound set in one of those long avenues that stretch south from Changan Street. This is the headquarters of the huge propaganda machine which distributes millions of copies of books, magazines, and pamphlets about Communist China to foreign countries. About three thousand people work for the press, and about a hundred of them work for the English-language editions. The place has grown so haphazardly and is so vast that people have to be taken by guides through a maze of corridors, tunnels, and courtyards, dimly lit and strangely silent at night. It was a little like entering a rabbit warren with hundreds of branching tunnels that lead to more branching tunnels. I went there on two successive nights and can only guess at the immensity of the place.

The man I went to see was a scholar and an eminent translator, quick and alert, though frail, with graying hair and penetrating eyes. He wore a faded blue Mao jacket which set off the grave beauty of his face. I had seen him last in Chungking thirty years ago when he wore a scholar's gown and walked gracefully across the campus of his university. Since he was very knowledgeable about writers, poets, and artists, I asked him to tell me about the men I had known long ago. Who was alive? Who was dead? Who was still writing? What had happened to the generation of poets who emerged during the war? Was any good literature being produced under communism? And most especially, what had happened to my friend Pien Chih-lin, a poet who had fought with the guerrillas and possessed a command of startling images, and to another friend Ai Ching, who had been called "the drummer of a new age."

There was a long silence as he collected his thoughts and memories together. It appeared that many were alive but few were writing. Pien Chih-lin had published nothing since the Communists came to power. He was thought to be teaching in a high school somewhere in Peking. Ai Ching had traveled to the northwest and written a long novel, which was not particularly good and would probably not be published. Feng Yu-lan, the author of a voluminous history of Chinese philosophy, was still at work revising his history and attempting to construct a bridge between Marxism and traditional Chinese philosophy. He was very old now and had cut off his beard. I remembered him as a tall, gaunt man with a long, wild, black, spidery beard, with blazing eyes and violent gestures. It appeared that he had been tamed and no longer made violent gestures.

So what had happened to Chinese literature?

"It exists," my friend said, "but it is not in very good shape."

"Why not?"

"It is easy to say: 'Why not?' It is much more difficult to find the reasons. Part of the reason clearly lies with Chiang Ching, who acquired extraordinary power over books, newspapers, films, operas, ballet, even painting. She ruled the arts with a heavy hand. She and her agents were everywhere. She had no taste and very little knowledge, and yet she dominated the entire scene. Now that she is in disgrace we can breathe again. The worst is over, and the thaw is coming."

"When?"

"Oh, it will take time. The machinery moves slowly— you have no idea how cumbrous the machinery is. We shall have to turn sharply in a different direction altogether but we still don't know what direction to take. Also, it is not entirely the fault of Chiang Ching. There were other factors. We still haven't succeeded in identifying them all. You must remember, too, that we are still in a state of shock. There is not the least doubt that she spread poison over literature and the arts, acting virtually as the dictator, but there is another and more important question to be answered. Why did we permit it to happen? Why was nothing done until it was almost too late? She left her mark on a whole generation of writers and artists, and ruined them!"

I said something about communism having no workable relationship with writers and artists. Communism had no place for them, since it demanded their absolute obedience and by nature they were not capable of obedience. In his speech at the Yenan Forum, Mao Tse-tung had announced that he would destroy all literature that did not place itself at the service of communism, and surely he was therefore responsible for the death of Chinese literature. There followed many years later his summons to let "the hundred flowers" bloom, but the flowers were not permitted to bloom. Why not? The government was strong, all-powerful, monolithic. Criticism could not harm it. It could indeed only strengthen it. Criticism was healthy, and if it had been permissible to criticize Chiang Ching, then her extraordinary elevation to dictator of the arts would never have happened.

He said: "You don't understand. This is not how things are in China."

"Did no one protest?"

He was silent for a while. It was clear that the protesters, if they existed, achieved very little. Chiang Ching was entrenched in her position of power; she was the wife of Mao Tse-tung; she would go to a conference of writers or to a factory and say "Chairman says this" or "Chairman says that," and no one would dare to dispute her. It was useless to appeal to Mao Tse-tung, for he was surrounded by her creatures.

"So in effect she was the ruler of China?"

"No, that is not true. We never thought of her in this way. She was something to be endured. There were other forces at work—the army, the bureaucracy, the party."

"But they all permitted her to exert her power?"

Again he made no reply. It was as though he was still bemused, still uncertain of the true shape of affairs. There were no easy answers, and he was indeed incapable of making easy answers. He had seen his friends imprisoned; his own wife had been arrested; some of his friends had vanished for years. He said: "She did more harm than anyone can imagine. Only now are we beginning to understand the full extent of it. You said just now that you could not understand the rage against her shown on the posters. Well, we have a right to feel rage against her, because she nearly destroyed the revolution."

He went on: "You may have heard of the American Roxane Witke, who was invited to write a book about her. This American was writing a study of prominent Chinese women in the revolution. She had interviews with many people and she was in Canton, leaving the country, when she received a telegram from Chiang Ching, telling her to wait there, there were important matters to discuss, please wait. She waited. Chiang Ching arrived by airplane with her entire retinue, with cameramen and tape recorders. She said to Miss Witke: 'I want you to tell the story of my life. You will be my Edgar Snow.' So they sat down together and for sixty hours Chiang Ching dictated the story of her life, beginning with her childhood, going on to her film career, her journey to Yenan, her marriage to Chairman Mao Tse-tung, and all the years afterward. It was an extraordinary performance. She planned it all very carefully. She brought documents which substantiated her story. She was absolutely determined that the story of her life should be known in America and in the rest of the world."

"Why?"

"Obviously she had her own reasons. Obviously she wanted to assert herself abroad. Perhaps, too, she wanted to publish it in Chinese after the death of Chairman Mao. Her book was a bid for fame, as though she did not have enough fame already."

"She may have been encouraged," I suggested, for Chinese intrigues have worked in this way for many centuries.

"I don't think she was encouraged. I think she desperately felt the need for a book proclaiming her own greatness. She claimed some surprising things. She claimed, for example, that she was responsible for Chairman Mao's ideas on literature delivered at the Yenan Forum. She claimed too that when Yenan was attacked by Chiang Kai-shek's forces, she was responsible for the strategies employed and the final evacuation. These were two very important claims among many others. She was presenting herself as a strategist and as an annunciator of doctrine. She was claiming things that no Chinese could possibly believe."

All the way across China from Canton to Peking there were those posters denouncing the Gang of Four in strident and ever more vociferous tones. Sometimes, in those strange, awkward, ugly sketches you saw a woman whose hair was bright yellow and who was therefore not Chinese receiving from Chiang Ching's hands a book or some documents. In these sketches Chiang Ching herself appeared in a long flowing skirt and wearing a crown. She was the empress, though she resembled a frog, and her three courtiers resembled insects. The Chinese text running across the posters proclaimed that she was committing treason by giving documents to a foreigner. I remembered particularly one of these sketches about two feet wide and four feet high pasted on the walls of Yo Fei's temple in Hangchow, Chiang Ching looking more froglike than ever and Miss Witke kneeling before her and shown as though she was avidly reaching out for the documents that were being presented to her. It was pure caricature, lucid, harsh, venomous, and curiously impressive in its simplicity and force. Chiang Ching's public trial was taking place on billboards all over China. Her own voice was silent and it was unlikely that it would ever be heard.

I asked him what he thought would happen to Chiang Ching, who was under arrest and being continually interrogated. It was generally assumed that her followers, once among the most privileged people in China and numbering many thousands, were also under arrest. He seemed to think that there would be a trial which would not be open to the public and a formal sentence would be handed down. He was reasonably certain she would not be executed but she would be effectively prevented from taking any further part in politics.

I said: "I remember reading that in the Yenan days the Chinese Communist leaders, remembering what happened after the French Revolution and the Russian Revolution, swore that they would not under any circumstances kill each other. They knew the dangers of splits and schisms. The punishment might be exile or imprisonment but never death."

"That is true," he replied. "They made a very solemn agreement and they kept to it. It is well attested, they have talked about it, and although quite probably there exists no document which specifically states in so many words that they will not under any circumstances kill each other, we are quite sure that they made an agreement of this kind."

"So that might help Chiang Ching?"

"Yes or no. You have to think of the gravity of her crimes. I cannot imagine she will be executed. As far as I am concerned, it is all over. She is finished and we can breathe again, and probably the less we think about her the better it will be."

We talked about books and propaganda, about magazines, about the lack of any real knowledge of the United States in China. It seemed to me that China had been appallingly served by her publicists. *Chinese Literature*, a monthly issued in hundreds of thousands of copies, was so lacking in imaginative literature that I could not remember a single memorable issue. There were short stories ascribed to peasants which quite obviously had not been written by peasants, or if so they had been worked over by so many hack writers that the original peasant story was completely obliterated. The stories were full of incomprehensible jargon. There was no life in the magazine, no hint of the genius of China which had surely survived the Chinese Communist Revolution. It was the same with the works written by foreigners at the invitation of the Chinese Communists. With the one remarkable exception of Edgar Snow's *Red Star over China*, written forty years ago, not a single book had come out of China which really reflected the grandeur and the agony of the Chinese Revolution, and this was written thirteen years before the Chinese Communists came to power. No great novelists, no great poets had emerged. Han Suyin continued to write adoringly about Mao Tse-tung, but this was not literature. Rewi Alley wrote journals about his travels through China, but the journals told you very little about China. They were privileged writers permitted to go wherever they pleased, and there was little to show for it. Something had gone terribly wrong. Perhaps it was the very fact that they were privileged which made it so difficult for them to write convincingly. In the arts and in letters China had become a cultural desert. Why?

I had thought he would be offended, but he was not. He agreed that something had gone terribly wrong, that *Chinese Literature* was a disaster, that there was a desperate need for change, and that it would come. He did not believe that the accumulated rubbish heaps of jargon would wither away, but he was convinced that the Chinese could and would improve the quality of their published literature.

Because he was so hopeful, I began to talk about something that had been long on my mind—an exchange of books between China and the United States. The exchange of a few books was surely a very simple thing. We in America would translate a few selected books from China, and the Chinese in turn would translate a few selected books by American authors.

I said: "We must get to know one another again. We must build bridges. Even if we cannot build a complete bridge, we can start building the first springing arches from each coast. We must know each others' minds. China and the United States are indissolubly linked together. We are natural allies even though we have different social systems. And yet at this particular moment in history there is really no communication between us. So let us begin with books, even a few books—"

"What kind of books?"

"Our novels—our best novels. Our poems—our best poems. Your novels and your poems, dramas, everything."

"Who is to judge them?"

"We decide together."

"No," he said, and his voice sounded very sharp and uncompromising.

"Surely it is worth attempting."

"As for your novels, or at least the novels we have seen, they will be incomprehensible to the Chinese. Sex, brutality, escape into fantasy, irresponsibility. It is incomprehensible that Americans publish these books. I have been reading Doctorow's *Ragtime*. Can you imagine us translating this book and offering it to be read by Chinese peasants? As far as I can see, there is nothing in American literature that we can use."

"Nothing?"

"We have looked very carefully. We find nothing except

sensationalism. We have a whole new generation brought up under socialism and disciplined to serve the people. We are not going to feed them with violence and sex, and your sensational novels would say nothing to them. We are thinking of translating *Huckleberry Finn*."

"Mark Twain died a long time ago. He doesn't represent present-day America."

"Perhaps not, but he represents an aspect of America which we regard as important. We could make an arrangement. We translate *Huckleberry Finn* and you translate the best of our short-story writer Lu Hsün. We want him to be better known because he represents for us all that is best in our society."

I said: "Lu Hsün died long before the Communists came to power. Are there no Communist writers worth reading?"

"Not yet. Not now. There will be—it is bound to come. There will be a thaw. We are all sure that it is coming, but it will come about slowly. We no longer have to obey Chiang Ching. There will be a new beginning. The hundred flowers will bloom again!"

"So nothing is settled yet?"

"No, nothing is settled, but there is hope—a vast hope."

It was still snowing when I left him an hour later. Peking was drowning in snow and ice, and it would be spring before the thaw began.

The Palace on the Shih Fu Ma Ta Chieh

When I was last in Peking I lived in a palace that had once belong to Hsiung Hsi-ling, a former prime minister of China, and later to his daughter, Hsiung Ting, who was my wife. The palace was said to have 240 rooms, though we never counted them, and consisted of a vast number of courtyards opening onto one another through moon gates. It was very hot during the summer I lived there, and we lived very quietly. Distant relatives of the prime minister lived in distant courtyards, and we rarely saw them. Hsiung Hsi-ling was dead, but the imprint of his mind and character could be felt in the small region of the palace where we lived.

He was a Hunanese from an obscure military family and became a government official in the only way possible in his time, by passing a civil service examination of excruciating difficulty. The ruling bureaucracy consisted exclusively of scholars who had passed this examination. In time he became viceroy of Manchuria and headed various ministries before being appointed prime minister in 1914 in the government of Yuan Shih-kai. Hsiung's cabinet earned some fame as a cabinet of the talents, independent of existing parties. The cabinet fell after eight or nine months, and thereafter he played many roles behind the scenes as an elder statesman. In 1937 the Japanese invited him to become the puppet prime minister of all the Chinese territories they had conquered, and so one night he slipped away from Peking in disguise and made his way to Hong Kong, where he died a few months later. He was a stocky, round-faced man with a goatee, famous for the orphanage he erected in the Western Hills and for his calligraphy rather than for his political career.

In the early years after the revolution of 1911 the customs of imperial China still remained, and Hsiung Ting could remember a time when petitioners making their way to an audience with the prime minister would crawl on their hands and knees from the gateway to the reception room, and when at last they were dismissed they would crawl backward until he could no longer see them. She also remembered that the gatekeeper made a fortune from bribes. Such things happened within living memory, and there are people living today in China who can remember when a Chinese army fought in the frontier regions with bows and arrows.

The story was told that Hsiung Hsi-ling bought the palace piecemeal from a descendant of one of the Iron-Capped Princes, who were sons of the emperor Chien Lung. When the descendant needed money, he would sell off a courtyard, or two or three courtyards. Finally, over a period of years, when he had gambled all his money away and sold off all the courtyards, he gave the title deeds to the prime minister, who permitted him to live in the palace as long as he pleased.

I remembered the palace well: the huge stone lions guarding the gateway in the shade of an enormous ginkgo tree, the latticed paper-covered windows, the quietness of the inner courtyards, the servants dressed in black who moved about silently in cotton slippers. I remembered the spaciousness of the courtyards and the narrowness of the small rooms surrounding them, with brocades hanging on the walls and the heavy blackwood furniture which seemed in some way to anchor those lightly constructed rooms, all wood and paper, to the earth. Even now I can walk through these rooms blindfolded, knowing where everything is, my Chinese paintings on the walls, my pens and papers and small ivory seal on my desk, and all the clutter of married life around me. We were divorced long ago, but Hsiung Ting was still living in Peking. I asked her what had happened to the old palace.

"I don't think you will recognize it," she said. "You can't go into it but you can see the outside. The Communists took it and very properly converted it into a school and then into a training academy, and now they say it is a factory."

The snow was falling as we drove in a taxi past the Palace of the Iron-Capped Prince. I remembered a wide tree-shaded road, but the trees had been cut down, and there were no stone lions, and there was no ornamental gateway. The high wall surrounding the palace had been breached at intervals, providing space for small shops. There was a noise like hammering, and I saw a forge glowing in the depths of one of the shops. I looked for the ginkgo tree, but it had vanished.

"What do you think of it?" she asked.

"I think it was better in the old days. I wish they had not cut into the walls."

"No," she said. "I like the noise and the hammering and the people crowding in the streets. It is real now. It wasn't real when we lived there."

I lowered the window of the taxi and looked out through the snow at a street I had known well and no longer recognized, while the noise and the hammering grew louder.

The Old Mao Tse-tung

This evening, driving outside the Forbidden City, I observed that the whole of the great square which contains the Palace of the People, the Revolutionary Museum, and the white cenotaph erected to commemorate the martyrs of the Revolution, has been fenced off. There is a long wooden wall, about six feet high, with guards stationed at intervals, and in the gathering dusk this strange line drawn across the square looks curiously ominous. Everyone knows why the wall has been erected, or at least they know that Chairman Hua Kuo-feng recently laid the foundation stone for a mausoleum which will contain the body of Mao Tse-tung enclosed in a coffin of translucent cryolite. Somewhere on the great square the mausoleum will arise, and since the authorities have already declared that the building will be designed in "the appropriate Chinese style," we may expect that there will be flaring tiled roofs and that it will resemble a small, jewellike Chinese palace.

I am all in favor of a mausoleum. History will place Mao Tse-tung among the great conquerors, among the men who shake nations to their foundations and set them on new and hitherto unsuspected courses. Such men from the beginning of their careers appear to be destined for amazing burials. Alexander the Great was also buried in a crystal casket, which may still exist beneath one of the mosques of Alexandria. Lenin lies in a crystal casket near the Kremlin wall and thousands of pilgrims come daily to see the body, or what they believe to be the body, of the man who brought about such vast changes in Russia. Yet it puzzles me a little that the Communists who claim to be such rigorously scientific materialists should have such regard for a leader's mortal flesh that they would want to display it long after his death. The official explanation is provided by a directive issued by the Central Committee of the Chinese Communist party. It is being done, says the directive, so that "his memory may be honored eternally" and so that "the great masses of the people will be able to offer him homage." Eternity and homage have a deeply religious connotation. He has slipped out of history and become a god.

What is gained by deification? I doubt whether anything is gained, because it is in the nature of things that deification will obscure his humanity, his human achievements. The man vanishes behind the oracle, the vigor vanishes in the static image. What was great in Mao Tse-tung was precisely his daring, his visionary belief that an age-old society could be overthrown, his absolute insistence on destroying it because it had outlived its usefulness. He ripped the ancient fabric apart, as though with his bare hands.

We learned recently that Chiang Ching protested vehemently against preserving his body, saying that it was his wish to be cremated, as Chou En-lai and Chu Teh were cremated. The Chinese government did not feel in any way bound by her words. Mao Tse-tung belonged to history and to legend, not to her. On this subject the government is quite adamant. The extraordinary campaign against the Gang of Four can be understood as an attempt to destroy Chiang Ching as a historical figure in her own right and also to silence her as the creator of new histories and new legends. I suspect that it is also an attempt to set back the clock to the days before the Great Proletarian Cultural Revolution swept over China with disastrous consequences, for in that strange revolution she played a major role.

In the dusk the Gate of Heavenly Peace possesses a great beauty, a great majesty. Those gates and walls, those marble balustrades and delicate cloud-columns of pure white stone form an abstract design of overwhelming power; it is as though power had been invented here and had its home behind those maroon-colored walls. Here, on a balcony above the gate, Mao Tse-tung sometimes reviewed processions of his worshipers a million strong. In the fading light, with snow falling, it was still possible to see the vast portrait of him hanging down from the balcony. In sunlight it glowed with bright colors but the dusk washed the colors away; and gradually as it grew darker the details of the face vanished until it was only a blur.

Within the Forbidden City, in a region called Chungnanhai, set amid lakes and gardens, Mao Tse-tung spent the last twenty-six years of his life. It was a strange world, unreal in its beauty, which belonged to the age of the

Ming emperors. A thousand armed guards protected the high officials whose homes and offices were small palaces with yellow-tiled roofs. In all seasons this area within the walls of the Forbidden City is filled with flowers. The yellow tiles were reflected in the lakes, the willows drooped gracefully, and in the summer came the explosion of pink lotuses. From the barren valley of Yenan the Chinese Communist leaders came to live amid the sumptuous elegance of the Forbidden City. It did not turn their heads, but it subtly altered their style and perhaps of all the leaders Mao Tse-tung was the one who was most deeply affected by his surroundings. As time passed, he became more regal, more imperious. He alone possessed the tablets of the law. He alone commanded. Once, shortly before the Great Proletarian Cultural Revolution, André Malraux said to him: "So you have become like one of the great emperors." Mao Tse-tung replied: "Of course," and went on to speak of more important things.

There were two Mao Tse-tungs. There was the man who said "We must trust the people—only the people" and the man who gave orders without consulting the people and without knowing what they were thinking. One looked to the past, the other to the future. Everything he accomplished on the road to power had a coherent logic, and his strength came from the people. Later he relied heavily on his own strength, his own fame, his own arbitrary judgment, approaching problems with an artist's intuition rather than with his human intelligence. And inevitably there was havoc, and inevitably China suffered from his highhandedness. Now that he is dead, I suspect that the highhandedness will be forgiven and forgotten and he will be remembered for his supremely human qualities.

One of his favorite books was *Journey to the West*, which told the story of an impudent monkey Sun Wu-kung, who had the power of being able to leap 108,000 leagues in a single bound. He performed prodigies of valor. He stormed the gates of hell in order to cross off his name from the Book of Fate. He ate the peaches of immortality in the gardens of paradise and he made a valiant attempt to storm heaven, and was such a nuisance that the Jade Emperor had to summon Buddha for assistance. Buddha was clever. He promised Monkey that the kingdom of heaven would be granted to him on one condition. Sitting in the palm of Buddha's hand he had only to jump clear away from the hand and he would be granted all his wishes. Nothing, thought the monkey, could be easier. He made one of his great leaps and found himself at the five-columned gate which he thought to be the end of the world. On one of these columns he wrote: "Great Sage Equal of Heaven has been here." Then, as a further reminder that he had been there, he urinated at the foot of another column before making another prodigious leap back into Buddha's palm. He immediately claimed all the palaces of heaven. "What a little fool you are," Buddha said kindly. "Where did you fly to?"

"To the end of the world," Monkey replied.

"No, you reached my fingers and no farther," Buddha said. "I observe that you left your mark on two of them."

Monkey continued to wage war on heaven. By a curious device he was able to multiply himself at will. All he needed to do was to pluck some hair from his body, bite it, cry out "Change!" and immediately there would be hundreds of monkeys waiting to do his bidding. The Chinese word for "hair" is *mao*. Sometimes during the Great Proletarian Cultural Revolution it must have seemed to Mao Tse-tung that he had multiplied to the utmost possible degree, that everyone was obedient to him, and that he had successfully stormed heaven, but in fact it was not so.

He was aging rapidly. The plotters and the mischief-makers were all round him, and he was not always capable of distinguishing good men from bad. The Shakespearian drama was played out to the end. His life was a triumph which ended in tragedy.

The snow continued to fall and Peking became a ghostly city in the darkness, and was all the more ghostly in the side streets where the little makeshift huts had been erected under the trees as a protection against earthquakes, for these huts were shapeless and yet they somehow gave the impression that an army was bivouacking in the streets. Yet even at night in the deep darkness that settles on Peking in winter, the city remained beautiful with the shapes of towers and palaces printed against the sky. The radio said that another earthquake was still expected and all precautions must continue to be maintained.

During the night the snow stopped falling, and shortly after dawn we flew on a Chinese airplane to Japan.

Mao Tse-tung in old age.

Descent into the tomb of the Ming emperor Wan Li.

Tomb of Emperor Wan Li.

Hall of Supreme Harmony, Peking.

The Gate of Heavenly Peace, Peking, under snow.

Bronze lions in Forbidden City.

A fabulous beast.

NOTES FROM A DIARY

Now that the journey to China is over, I feel a sense of exaltation because we were able to see so much, and at the same time there is a sense of regret that we were not allowed to stay longer, that we were not allowed to see many of the people we wanted to see, that we were cabined and confined too closely. We were well aware that the Chinese government must keep watch on visitors, but was it necessary to keep watch on us all the time?

We made lists of names of the people we wanted to see, gave them to our guides, and hoped for the best. Most of the people I had known in China years ago were in Peking. They included Hsiung Ting; Professor Chen Dai-sen, who was head of the economics department of Peking University; Professor Shen Yu-ting of the Institute of Philosophy; Dr. George Hatem, the veteran American doctor who had built up the cave hospitals in Communist territory and whom I had known in the Yenan days; Madame Soong Ching-ling, the widow of Dr. Sun Yat-sen, who had once given me a message to transmit to Jawaharlal Nehru; and several others. I was told it was absolutely impossible to see Professor Shen Yu-ting, Dr. Hatem, and Madame Soong. No reasons were given. The worst was not seeing Madame Soong, who was the last person I saw in China thirty years ago. Adorably beautiful, she represented in her person the living history of China during all these tumultuous decades, the one bright constant star in the firmament. I sent her a copy of a book I had written and wrote in it how much I regretted not seeing her.

These rejections seemed to be quite arbitrary. A request was regarded as a petition, and an obscure bureaucrat decided whether the petition should be granted. It was infuriating and there was absolutely nothing I could do about it.

For two years at the National Southwest University in Kunming in southwest China I lived in one of the boxes of a theater belonging to an old warlord. Dr. Chen Dai-sen lived in another box, and there were about ten of us, all professors at the university, who took our meals regularly in the theater at a large round blackwood table facing the empty stage. Tall, long-faced, very pale, speaking English with a Harvard accent, Dr. Chen presided over the table with irony and good humor. He was the leading economist in China and wore his learning lightly, and he thought I was mad because I enjoyed translating Chinese poetry, a task that was demonstrably impossible, and that my friend Shen Yu-ting was madder, because as a philosopher he seriously believed that it was possible through philosophy to unravel the secrets of the universe. I found him little changed, though the irony had grown sharper with the passing years. He had retired from his position as head of the department of economics, but no successor could be found, and so he had resumed his duties with reluctance. It appeared that there were very few students and his duties were not arduous.

He talked about the epic march of the Peking universities to Kunming during the war against Japan. One group under Wen Yi-tuo made the long journey on foot, while others reached Kunming by circuitous routes, some by way of Hong Kong, others by way of Hanoi, and still others by even more adventurous routes. National Southwest University consisted of about twenty wooden cattle sheds erected outside the north gate of the city in an abandoned cemetery. I remembered Dr. Chen striding up to the north gate in his long blue gown. Now he wore an immaculate black Mao uniform tightly buttoned at the neck. I asked him whether the turmoil of recent years had affected his views of economics and how it was possible that the Chinese economy could have remained so stable. He answered that the Chinese economy remained stable because it answered the needs of the people and his views of economics had not changed because he was concerned chiefly with the history of economics and not with theory. Chinese economics was pragmatic, and the economy of China was much simpler than, for example, the economy of the United States. It was therefore easier to manage and presented fewer problems.

Professors in China are usually well paid. He said his salary was 370 yuan a month, and he paid 14 yuan a month for a large house.

So we talked through the evening over cups of green tea in one of the gilded reception rooms of the Peking Hotel, basking in Communist luxury. Under the Kuomintang we had lived in grotesque poverty in an abandoned theater, where the roof leaked, the timbers were rotting, and there was scarcely room to move about in our little boxes.

There was a tremendous fuss at the airport.

We reached it very early as dawn was breaking, shivering with cold. The sky was overcast, there were rumors that the flight would be delayed, and we were preparing for a long wait. Suddenly there was an announcement that we should go immediately to customs. We carried our heavy luggage along concrete passageways, filled out forms, changed Chinese money back into American money, and submitted our luggage for inspection. Only my luggage was inspected. The inspectors tore into it, turned everything upside down, ordered the Chinese scrolls I had bought to be unrolled, looked at every book, examined dirty socks and crumpled shirts and the lining of the suitcases, and every moment they were becoming more urgent, more red-faced, more determined to find contraband.

Finally they found it—a *ting* two inches high, a bronze bowl supported on three tiny legs, very delicate and beautiful. I had bought it for sixty dollars in a Tsingtao department store. "It has no red seal," the customs inspector said. "It is a national treasure. You cannot take it away." I explained that it was not a national treasure, it was no more than a hundred years old, and objects in department stores do not have red seals attached to them. He was adamant. "The national treasure remains here," he said. As I ran to the airplane, the little green tripod still sat on the customs counter.

Speaking to some visitors in the fall of 1976, the widow of Chou En-lai said: "Nothing that ever happened in China was so terrible as what happened this year between April and October." It was a strange and revealing statement by someone who had been close to the centers of power. She was a revolutionary in her own right, an intelligent and forthright woman who was not given to exaggeration, and she was not talking only about the earthquake or the deaths of Chou En-lai, Chu Teh, and

Mao Tse-tung, the three undisputed captains of the Chinese Communist Revolution, although all these disasters were implicated in her statement. One thought of the many calamities that have affected China through the ages—the floods that drowned whole provinces, the massacres of millions of Chinese by invaders, the epidemics that raged unchecked and carried more millions to their graves. These things had happened repeatedly; they were terrible beyond belief; but in 1976 there were no floods, no invasions, no epidemics. An earthquake had shattered a large mining town near Peking, but Peking herself remained virtually undamaged. There was a functioning government, and its orders were being obeyed in far-distant provinces. There was no unemployment, no inflation, the shops were full of goods, and the revolution was pursuing its charted course. Then why was she saying: "Nothing that ever happened in China was so terrible as what happened this year between April and October"?

I suspect that she knew what she was saying and that she had good reasons for saying it. In those months China suffered shock after shock, but they were not all registered on the Richter scale. Some were psychological shocks administered on a patient who scarcely knew what was happening, who had no means to combat them, and who knew obscurely that treachery and conspiracy were abroad and that all the vast and intricate underpinnings of the state were in danger of collapse not because they were decaying but because somewhere in the heart of the government an effort was being made to destroy them. Long ago Sun Yat-sen had described China as "a sheet of shifting sand," and he despaired of ever bringing purpose and unity to the state. Purpose and unity had been given to China by the Communist Revolution and achieved at a great cost in lives and suffering. There was a dreadful suspicion seeping through the country that things were going terribly wrong and that it might be beyond human capacity to set them right again. People asked themselves who would leap into the vacuum of power caused by the deaths of the three leaders within a few months of each other; and while the official newspapers proclaimed that the nation was stable and under control, there was the sense that the center could not hold and that anarchy might be loosed upon China.

We are beginning to realize that the campaign against Chiang Ching reflects the fears and anxieties of the period between April and October, when there were shadowy conspiracies and intrigues around Mao Tse-tung's deathbed. Out of respect for Mao Tse-tung the people acquiesced to his long silences, but the silence at the end of his life was more difficult to bear. The ancient Chinese historians Pan Ku and Ssu-ma Chien have sometimes described at great length the conspiracies that accompanied the deaths of medieval emperors. Usually these secret battles for the succession were short and sharp; they took place behind high walls, and they ended like Shakespearian tragedies. Kingly power, unless the principles of succession are clearly established, lends itself to these dangerous quarrels. What is surprising is that the Chinese Communist leadership did not grasp the necessity for a simple, clearly stated formula for the succession. When Mao Tse-tung died everything had to begin again.

In the democracies power moves easily from one president to another, one prime minister to another. But in the Chinese Communist state all power is centered on the Chairman and a small body of officials chosen by him. The transfer of power can come about only when the Chairman has given his blessing to his successor and when the successor receives the acclamation of the people. Hence the importance of the brief message in which Mao Tse-tung declared he would rest happy if he knew that Hua Kuo-feng would be his successor, and also of the massive parades in which the new Chairman was acclaimed by the people of Peking. But this was evidently not the whole story. We do not know what other messages came from the dying Chairman, and we can only guess at the fierce infighting that took place. The arrest and imprisonment of Chiang Ching on October 6, 1976, may have been only a small incident in the struggle.

In this way, as so often in Chinese history, we learn what has happened only in part. We learn by sifting rumors, from silences and hesitations. We learn from the lips of wise old women as much as from official proclamations. We learn by watching the leaves fall from the trees and from the strange colorings of the sky.

We had only one long conversation with our guides about the Russians. In 1960 Khrushchev withdrew all Soviet aid to Communist China, including about eight thousand engineers. The Sino-Soviet Friendship Pact was canceled, and as a result China suffered severe economic losses. Mao Tse-tung declared that henceforth the Chinese would be self-reliant and be the better for it. Why, we asked, had all this come about?

The guide said: "Because the Russians are deviationists following the capitalist road."

"Yes," we said, "but the Americans are also deviationists who follow the capitalist road. Exactly what does 'following' mean? Who follows what? Surely there are some Russians who are not following this road. Surely not all Russians are capitalists?"

"They are following the capitalist road," the guide said stubbornly.

"What does that mean exactly?"

"It means that they are not Socialists, they are not Communists. They have abandoned Marxism-Leninism-Stalinism. They have joined the capitalists."

"You mean the Americans?"

"Yes, they act like Americans."

"But you say you like the Americans and admire our industrial progress?"

"It is not the same thing. We are against the Russians because they have stolen our land and because they betrayed us. We have a large army on the frontier between China and the Soviet Union. We do not have a large army on the frontier of China and America—"

So it went on, the same circuitous argument we had had the previous day and would probably have the following day. He had not been given the proper line concerning the appropriate current attitude toward the Soviet Union: he held fast to the things he knew—hatred, betrayal, following the capitalist road. He seemed lost and confused. There was Russia, vast, menacing, armed with ten thousand atomic warheads, confronting China which has perhaps no more than a dozen atomic warheads; and in all his answers there was an unspoken fear of Russia. Among the Russians, too, there was a deep-seated fear of China. This was expressed by the poet Andrey Voznesensky in a poem written at the time of the Great Proletarian Cultural Revolution:

> *I feel them.*
> *I feel those Asian barbarians.*
> *Through all their nonsensical talk about*
>   *the communes*
> *China's God of War*
> *Rises from the mushroom cloud.*

Will our cosmonauts return from Mars
To find the barbarian Chinese in control?

Could it be that Shakespeare and Stravinsky
Will be dragged along howling streets
With garbage cans over their heads?

We have known blond Supermen
Who skinned babies for lampshades:
Now the Super-East dreams of skinning
    the West,
And China means war.

Pray for Russia!
Save Russia from the Asian hordes!
Under the cosmic drizzle
The earth covers its shoulders with Russia
And shivers.

The raw hatred in the poem tells us a good deal about the Russian attitude toward the Chinese, but the Chinese attitude toward the Russians is more complex, for they prefer to pretend that Russia does not exist. Fear, the sense of loss, betrayal: all these. But there is also, I believe, a deep feeling that these storms will blow over in time and meanwhile the Chinese are determined to guard their frontiers with every man they can spare. They have no illusions about the Russians and they are far from believing that the United States is their natural ally. They know too that with her unnumbered millions China will survive, if any country survives.

Some weeks later there came a letter from Peking written in bright blue ink with festoons of orange stamps on the envelope. It read:

Please accept my deep appreciation for your *Chinese Diaries* which brings to mind many important events during the Japanese aggression, particularly your part in presenting my appeal to Jawaharlal Nehru to send doctors and relief supplies. We had hardly any medicines and the morale was low. Mr. Nehru immediately sent us a medical mission with some medicines. I was so touched that I went down to welcome them in Canton.

This has been a very sad year for us—the loss of three great leaders, and the wicked gang who tried to seize leadership. Indeed, the experiences of the year past make us all more and more aware how subject we seem to be to the unforeseen and the unforeseeable!

I am leaving for my home in Shanghai to get some treatment for my rheumatism caused by this wretched dry weather here. I hope to be back in three months if nothing needs my presence here. With my deep appreciation and warm regards,

> Yours sincerely,
> Soong Ching-ling

EPILOGUE: JAPAN

A Riot of Temples

In Peking it was winter, the snow falling, the icy winds blowing across the Mongolian plains, and the palaces with their yellow roofs were transformed into palaces of snow and ice, but in Kyoto it was still autumn with the trees still green, not yet turned to yellow and orange. On the bullet train from Tokyo we were told it was unlikely we would see Mount Fuji, for in this season of the year it was often covered with clouds, but as the train swept past it the clouds suddenly rolled away and for perhaps thirty seconds we saw the mountain in all her glory, white and glowing, naked, like a beautiful woman who has let her gown fall from her shoulders. It was like magic, like an apparition high in the air. If it had happened less suddenly, we might have felt cheated.

And in Kyoto it was the same: sudden perfection met us on so many roads that we came to expect it, to regard it as normal and inevitable. There were temples ablaze with the fiery sculptures of the twelfth century and with the paintings of the Kano school five hundred years later.

There were gardens where the stepping stones were works of art and other gardens where four or five stones stood amid the raked sand, and you could imagine whatever you liked—the stones were islands in the sea or constellations in the heavens—and always the imagination played upon them with a sense of liberation. The perfect stones lay in their perfect fields of sand. It was ridiculous, but it was also true that the stones were formidable sculptures. Above all there were the carvings of Buddha made during the high tide of religious feeling to haunt us with their beauty and authority. We came under the ancient Japanese spell.

The original group that flew from America to Hong Kong had dispersed. There were only four of us in Japan— Johnny Fairchild, his wife Beatrice, Harry Schwartz, and myself. Professor Fairchild and I walked slowly through Kyoto, while Beatrice Fairchild, a biochemist with an international reputation, eager to see all things in the twinkling of an eye, marched far in advance, and Harry Schwartz, being younger, outdistanced us all. As a town planner, he saw the towns as organic creations which grew according to natural law, developing their own elaborate defenses and immunities. The rest of us were more inclined to see towns as faces, colors, street signs, temples, and monuments. We knew nothing or very little about town-making and he knew everything that could be known.

On the second or third day in Kyoto we discovered that China was beginning to recede into the past—into the distant past. In China we had been herded like sheep, but in Japan we were free to go where we pleased, we could talk to anyone we pleased, and if we asked a question we received an answer that was not heavy with sarcasm or totally irrelevant or simply: "Chairman Mao Tse-tung says . . ."

We reveled in our newfound freedom. We went to the

Kabuki theater, which was just as stylized as Peking opera, but more urgent and more colorful than the posturings on the Chinese stage. We especially watched the young Japanese in the streets, boys and girls walking arm in arm, the boys in jeans and the girls in skirts. They laughed a good deal, and we had forgotten the sound of laughter. China was masculine, authoritarian, heavy-handed, while Japan was feminine, the government weighed lightly on the people, and there were no street committees to watch over the comings and goings of all the residents. The Chinese had embraced a puritanical morality apparently without realizing that puritanical behavior introduces intolerable frustrations. The Japanese had evolved a civilization in working order, where it was inconceivable that a Chiang Ching could arise to torment a whole generation of writers and artists, and where people were ceremonious and behaved kindly toward one another.

Above all there were the temples, those museums of Japan's ancient past, where the past went on living, not by permission of the government but with its own momentum, its own assurance. Here the ancient gods were still living and there were no commandments to prevent them from blessing the people.

Conversation with a Green Dragon

In Japan, and especially in Kyoto, the strangest things are likely to happen and no one raises an eyebrow. Thus it happened that one afternoon while I was meditating beside the small lake in front of the Golden Pavilion, a green dragon emerged from a forest of cryptomeria trees, rested himself firmly on his haunches, drew his knees up to his chin, coiled his long green glittering tail around the pavilion and began one of those conversations in which he always permitted himself the last word. He was a familiar friend, I had known him since my childhood, and he had a pleasant habit of appearing and disappearing when least expected.

"I hear you have just been to China," he began. "You went coughing and roaring all the way up the coast from Canton to Peking in the middle of winter. Tell me, did you enjoy it?"

"I enjoyed every moment."

"Good, you have made a precise statement. This can be proved or disproved as in a court of law. You say you enjoyed it. Here is a photograph of you wearing a yellow woolen cap pulled nearly over your eyes while you are standing morosely on the edge of a cabbage field. Do you recognize yourself?"

"Certainly."

"What have you to say in your defense?"

"It was on a commune—"

"Are you saying that you disapprove of communes?"

"No."

"Then what were you disapproving?"

"The chairman of the revolutionary committee."

"Why?"

"He was telling us how many cabbages were grown per hectare and how many man-hours were spent in raising how many cabbages."

"So you disapprove of the communes?"

"My grandfather fought in the French Commune in 1871. He died before I was born, but I am devoted to his memory. Since he fought in the first of all communes I am inclined to believe there may be some good in them."

"A cautious answer, but it avoids the main issue. It is

clear from the photograph that you wished you were somewhere else. You look as though you were in agony."

"I was."

"Tell the court exactly why you were in agony."

"I have already told you. I was getting very tired of
people who call themselves chairmen of revolutionary
committees. They talked too much. They got more money
than the workers. They acted like bureaucrats. Mao Tse-
tung hated them too, so you cannot accuse me of being
against the Chinese Communists. I did not like the guides
very much because they spoke in Chinese Communist jargon. Mao Tse-tung also hated jargon."

"So you are on the side of Mao Tse-tung against the
bureaucrats?"

"I suppose so."

"But the bureaucrats were directly or indirectly appointed by Mao Tse-tung and owed their power to him?"

"True."

"Do you observe any inconsistency in your statement?"

"None whatsoever."

"Does it occur to you that Mao Tse-tung was also a
bureaucrat in his own way?"

"Yes."

"And so you are stating a preference for one set of
bureaucrats over another set?"

"Not exactly."

"I can see that we shall not progress very far along this
line. Tell me, you have written a fairly lengthy account of
your journey in China with many recorded conversations,
and I must therefore assume that you have an excellent
memory?"

"Yes."

"Admirable. You remind me of Matteo Ricci, the Jesuit
priest in the court of the emperor Wan Li. He would ask

one of the courtiers to pick out ten pages of the Chinese Classics. He would read the ten pages rapidly, shut the book, and immediately he would recite the ten pages aloud. The Chinese emperor was very impressed. Do you remember your conversation with Lao Wu in Shanghai?"

"Of course."

"You took notes, I suppose?"

"Yes."

"Detailed notes?"

"No, I scribbled a few things like 'room, upstairs, four flights.' "

"I notice that you fleshed out your conversations at some length—"

"Good, I am glad you noticed it."

"You are being impertinent. You were also impertinent in China. You asked questions when it would have been more polite to remain silent. You sometimes carried impertinence to extremes. You might have learned more if you had been less impertinent."

"We did not learn very much from our questions."

"What did you learn from?"

"The scenery, the faces, the way people walked in the streets, and then how clean it was, and the excellent medical care, and the plentifulness of food."

"Is it your conclusion that the Chinese Communists are here to stay?"

"Of course."

"As they are now?"

"No, there will be great changes and they will come soon. There will be more incentives for the workers, more liberty for writers and artists, more tolerance. It is all cut-and-dried now and there is the realization that they have been standing still and it is time for them to move on again. The dogmas are wearing thin. They will have to find new dogmas, new directions. Governments must be in a continual process of change, or else they die. For too long the government has been fossilized. Now they must go in search of a new form of communism with a human face."

"And do you really believe that the idea of communism with a human face has ever occurred to them?"

"Yes."

"For how long?"

"Since the death of Mao Tse-tung, when they were forced to realize that Mao's era was over and an entirely new direction has to be taken and a new helmsman has to be appointed. They are getting rid of the past—that is why the arrest of Chiang Ching and her followers is so important. They are aware that terrible mistakes have taken place and they are beginning to put their house in order. They know the direction they have to take—toward a greater freedom, toward a greater respect for the person, toward a softening of the harsh edges of bureaucracy. Soon, much sooner than we expect, they will begin to jettison the rubbish of the past and bring about communism with a human face."

"As for myself," said the dragon, "I am a very cynical old China Hand. I remember that Dr. Sun Yat-sen said the Chinese people were so ignorant that they needed to be kept under tutelage for a period of about fifty years before they could be trusted to govern themselves. There is always somone in China who says: 'You cannot be trusted, leave everything to me.' The dictator takes power and everyone bows his head and says: 'I submit, do whatever you like, we are sheep and will follow you blindly.' That is how it has been and how it will always be."

"I disagree. You are absolutely wrong. China is going to change rapidly from now on!"

"You're entitled to your opinion," the dragon said as he began to unwind his tail. "Good luck. But if you will take the advice of a very old dragon, you will hedge your bets."

Saying this, he swam across the lake with leisurely strokes and returned to his hiding place among the cryptomeria trees.

The Invisible Presences

Kyoto and Peking must be among the most difficult places in the world to tear oneself away from. There are so many temples, so many works of art, so many museums and gardens and parks that you can spend a month simply going from one to another without staying long enough to absorb what you have seen. You are caught in a maze of magnificence. In Kyoto especially there is the temptation to abandon everything else and to remain until the very last temple has been seen because this last temple may contain the supreme work of art that will explain all the other works of art. Here, hidden away in obscure temples, are paintings and sculptures of such dazzling perfection that you find yourself wondering how it is possible that they are not better known. In Kyoto the Japanese art of ten centuries has been preserved intact, and this is all the more remarkable because Japan is a country where earthquakes, conflagrations, and hurricanes are the commonplaces of life.

With difficulty we tore ourselves away from Kyoto and took the bullet train to Tokyo. Mount Fuji lay hidden in her clouds, but the sun shone over Tokyo and winter was beginning to sharpen the outlines of the city. One day we went to the puppet theater facing the imperial palace beyond the Sakurada moat. White gulls were flying overhead. We stood in line for the tickets, which are never easy to obtain, and thought ourselves lucky when we found seats in the last row. The puppet theater, known as *bunraku*, has an ancient history but in its modern form is not more than two hundred years old. The puppets are about two feet high and each one is manipulated by three men, so complex are the mechanical workings of the wooden face, hands, and feet. The puppets perform on a full-length stage, and to one side, on a platform detached from the stage, a singer and a *samisen* player sit cross-legged in front of a gold screen. The singer chants in a rather raucous and penetrating voice all the speeches of the puppets and the *samisen* player accompanies the action, playing violently during the battle scenes or when there are loud arguments from the puppets and softly when he wants to suggest a mood of gentleness. The singer and the *samisen* player are dressed in the uniform of the ancient court, they sit side by side, and are in such perfect harmony that they seem not to be two people but two aspects of one person. The puppets perform but their voices come from twenty feet away.

Bunraku is an art of extraordinary purity which has developed its own repertoire and its own conventions. Since the words are chanted and not always easy to understand, the Japanese often bring the text with them, studying it during the performance. The puppet masters—there may be fifteen of them on the stage at any one time—are clothed in black and wear black hoods over their faces. They are supposed to be invisible. The puppets are brightly painted, wear extravagantly rich costumes, and are designed to attract attention by the brilliance of their colors. And gradually, as the play continues, these small puppets become real people larger than life. The manipulators do their work well. Each jointed finger of the puppets can be made to move, mouths open, eyebrows are raised, knees bend, hands grasp swords and wield them, and there is the illusion that every part of the body is in motion. In fact these puppets are merely heads, arms, and feet, and there is nothing underneath the embroidered clothes.

We watched a procession of courtiers who came on an embassy to a prince, bearing gifts. They bowed low to the ground, declaimed their undying loyalty, offered their gifts, and moved elegantly across the brightly lit stage. It was clear that they were engaged in intrigues and were already suspect. They were denounced and threatened; they huddled together, commiserated with one another, and were finally permitted to leave the prince's presence. And then the prince spoke to his ministers and together they elaborated stratagems by which the ambassadors would fall into a trap. And so it went on. For a while I was entranced by the spectacle, the extraordinary brilliance and accuracy of the movements of the puppets, the repetitive music of the *samisen*, the strange raucous voice of the man who was chanting. The black-clothed, black-hooded puppet masters seemed to be invisible as they moved across the stage, or at least one paid no attention to them. After a while I forgot the play and saw only the puppet masters who lumbered across the stage, nearly shapeless, preposterously ugly, terrible in their awkwardness as they crowded round the puppets, one pulling the strings that operated the face, another pulling the strings that operated the arms and fingers, and the third pulling the strings that operated the legs. They bent low, but they were always at least twice the height of the diminutive, jewellike figures. They were invisible, and only too visible. They moved jerkily, while the puppets moved with an easy grace.

There came a moment of the purest horror when it seemed that the puppets were living people who were being manipulated by huge dark shadowy figures possessing absolute power over them. In the hands of the puppet masters the people were helpless; they could only obey. Like dark ghosts, like specters, these giantlike forms paraded their power and their subtle influences. They were faceless and obscene, and perhaps they knew nothing and perhaps they knew everything. There was no comfort in them: only the most bitter realization that perhaps after all we live under the dispensation of similar dark presences.

It seemed to me then, and seems to me now, that this was a kind of allegory of our time. The task before us is to free the living puppets from their masters, the Chiang Chings and all the other invisible forces who dominate our lives and pollute our imaginations. Our freedom depends on discovering who they are and rooting them out, and unless this is done we shall never be free again.

ACKNOWLEDGMENTS

I would like to thank Mr. John Trinkl, the leader of the *Guardian* Friendship Tour, for his many courtesies. I would also like to thank Professor John Fairchild, Dr. Beatrice Fairchild, Mr. Harry Schwartz, Mr. John Lennon, and Miss Sally Emory for their wonderful companionship at all times during the journey.

INDEX